THE JOURNEY

By

Rick Brown

To Bev, Reese and Grant:

You make my journey one of inexpressible joy.

TABLE OF CONTENTS

Chapter 1

Prologue

Each believer should be thirsting for God, for the living God, and longing to climb the hill of the Lord, and see Him face to face. We ought not to rest content in the mists of the valley when the summit awaits us. My soul thirsteth to drink deep of the cup which is reserved for those who reach the mountain's brow. Rest no longer satisfied with thy dwarfish attainments, but press forward to things more sublime and heavenly. Aspire to a higher, a nobler, a fuller life. Upward to heaven! Nearer to God! [1]

1. Charles H. Spurgeon, Morning and Evening: Daily Readings (Hendrickson Publishers, Inc., 1995), 657.

* * * * *

The vessel steamed through the day and deep into the night. Sam couldn't sleep, so he slipped on his deck shoes and jacket, and walked to the bow of the ship. Leaning on the rail, he took a spot among a few other restless travelers. No one spoke. Like the others, he strained to see something, anything in the vast darkness. The warm day had offered no hint of the evening chill, now made even more pronounced by the mist shooting up from below as the boat sliced almost noiselessly through the water.

After about thirty minutes, the first glimpse of light appeared in the distance, an intermittent luminance obscured and then revealed by the rise and fall of the sea. In another few minutes, however, the glow became more constant, reaching upward to form a faint umbrella over the horizon. For a while, it seemed to come from one source, but then each blink of the eye revealed more and more individual units of light as a city slowly began to take shape in the middle of the dark coastline. In unforced unison, the journeyers leaned forward on the rail and gazed silently toward their chosen destination.

* * * * *

A few days earlier…

Sam shuddered with a mix of excitement and apprehension. His twentieth birthday loomed, and he had decided to take the journey. This was not an unexpected decision, although it should be noted that most did not take the journey. Many young people Sam's age talked about it, but very few ever actually embarked on it. And in his town, it seemed like the majority of those who started the journey eventually wandered back, largely unchanged by the experience.

Sam actually knew very little about the specifics of the journey. He simply knew that he would be traveling to far away places, and experiencing new things. He assumed that the journey would be filled with adventure, and, he hoped, discovery, not only about these new and exotic places, but perhaps more importantly, about himself. Rumors of both grandeur and danger often swirled about whenever the topic was broached.

Sam walked briskly down the town's main street, taking care of the items on his last-minute checklist. He spotted the hardware store and headed in that direction. Gathered on the sidewalk in front of the store was the usual crew of late afternoon gossipers, engaged in lively conversations about the local news, the weather, and a variety of other topics that fill small town streets. As he approached, Sam sensed that the topic of the day was his decision to go on the journey. Gathered in a tight circle, the group's whisperings suddenly stopped as they turned in unison to stare at Sam as he walked by. Sam smiled politely. The mystique of the journey didn't bother him. Instead, it had become a major part of its appeal.

One thing annoyed Sam, however. Lately, a lot of the older folks in the town wanted to offer "advice," which, of course, means that they mostly wanted to talk about themselves and defend whatever decision they had made about the journey in their own lives.

On cue, a member of the circle called out, "I hope you know what you're doing, Sam. This journey thing—it don't amount to much except a lot of wasted time if you ask me."

Sam managed to keep his smile as he replied, "Well, maybe mine will be different, Mr. Benton." He wanted to call him by the name most people referred to him as—Bad News Benton—but he held his tongue.

"Ah, leave the boy alone," protested another member of the circle, a Mr. Johnson. "I did the journey myself and it was extraordinary. The things I did—you wouldn't believe all of it if I told you."

"You're right about that! I don't believe a word of it," shot back Mr. Benton.

Sam maintained his grin. "Thanks for your interest. I'll see all of you later and let you know all about it," Sam shouted back over his shoulder, never breaking his brisk stride.

Such direct comments from near-strangers were unusual, but Sam knew that many shared Mr. Benton's feelings. The ones who had never taken the journey, by far the vast majority, ridiculed those who had. "Just look at them. They're no different than any of the rest of us," they declared. But those few who had long ago embarked on the journey told grand (usually exaggerated, Sam thought) stories. Sam often wondered why, if their journey had been so great, they ended up back here, shuffling through the motions like everyone else. Sam also noticed something in common from both sets of people. No matter what their opinion or how passionately they spoke, Sam could see the shadows of longing and regret in their eyes.

Sam made quick time in the hardware store and crossed the items off his checklist. He needed to make just one more stop—the athletic supply store next door. As he entered and walked past the shopping carts, he saw the one man in the town who was somehow different than all the others—Mr. Spencer. Mr. Spencer rarely spoke about himself except in the most humble terms. He listened more than he talked, and he asked questions with genuine interest. Sam, despite his relative youth, knew that Mr. Spencer possessed something unique. At first he wasn't quite sure what it was, but one day it came to him. Mr. Spencer had a sparkle in his eyes that most of the others didn't. That was puzzling to Sam. The townsfolk often talked in hushed tones about "poor Mr. Spencer." Sam didn't know all the details, but this middle-aged man had apparently lost his family in some sort of accident a few years ago. Sam wasn't sure. All he knew was that Mr. Spencer's eyes seemed more penetrating, and they glinted with depth and emotion that Sam rarely saw in anyone else.

In spite of the way most people viewed Mr. Spencer, Sam didn't really think of him as the object of pity or sympathy. In fact, he seemed genuinely optimistic, and was the sort of person who always seemed to be helping someone else. He was kind and generous, although he did not appear to be wealthy, and Sam could tell there was a quality of integrity about Mr. Spencer that went beyond the petty comparisons and bickering that characterized so many others.

They exchanged greetings, and Mr. Spencer's eyes sparkled as he enthusiastically said, "I hear you're going on the journey."

"Yeah, I guess word gets around," Sam laughed.

"Are you ready?"

"I think so. I'll be leaving tomorrow," Sam answered. Then, acting on impulse and phrasing the question before he thought it through, Sam asked, "Didn't you go on the journey a long time ago?"

Mr. Spencer's smile widened, and Sam quickly continued. "I'm sorry; I didn't mean *that* long ago. I just meant, well, you know, when you went—um, *if* you went."

"I know you didn't mean anything negative, Sam," laughed Mr. Spencer. Then with eyes even more vibrant, he added, "Yes, I did go on the journey, but I was actually several years older than you are now, so it wasn't as long ago as you might suspect."

Sam's curiosity immediately eclipsed any worries that he had offended the older man. "Really? Not many older people go, do they?" he asked.

"You're right about that, Sam. I think it's best to take the journey when you're young and open to new experiences. It's harder if you're older. People get more—what's the word—rigid in their thoughts, stuck in a pattern. Adventure sounds great, but life tends to crowd it out the older you get. But anyone can go if they want."

"What was it like?"

Without hesitation, Mr. Spencer answered, "It changed my life."

"Really?" Sam quickly replied.

Mr. Spencer nodded. "Sam, the journey is not always easy. It can be hard and lonely, and some people, maybe most people, give up before they experience the best parts of it, but if you see it through it can be pretty amazing." For a moment Mr. Spencer was silent and his eyes seemed to drift to a distant place. Shifting his focus back to Sam, he continued, "But don't base anything on what I say. You'll experience it for yourself, and I hope it will be as life-changing for you as it was for me."

Sam glanced down at his watch. "I wish I had more time to talk, but I still have to pack a few more things before I leave tomorrow. If we'd only had this conversation earlier..." His voice trailed off momentarily, and then he continued, "There's so much mystery about the journey. It would have been good to hear your story."

"I understand, Sam, but everyone's journey is unique," Mr. Spencer smiled, and then said, "You have a great attitude. I think you'll be just fine." He hesitated for a moment, and then added, "Sam, I just want you to know"—another pause—"I'll be praying for you."

Sam did one of those verbal stumbles, like tripping over your own feet, only he tripped on his tongue. "Uh, that's cool. Thanks." He felt a little embarrassed, and he didn't quite know how to respond. Eventually Sam stuck out his right hand, and they shook and did the pat on the arm thing that guys often do with their free hand. "Take care," smiled Mr. Spencer, "and enjoy the journey."

"Yeah, see you around," Sam said, and then turned away to continue his last minute preparations.

Sam thought about the phrase Mr. Spencer had uttered as he left the store. "He'll be praying for me. I guess that's cool," Sam said to himself. Most people said something more generic, like "I'll be thinking about you," or perhaps, "our thoughts and prayers are with you." Sam had even used that one a time or two, although he didn't consider himself very religious, nor could he recall a time when he had actually prayed, except for reciting grace before a meal. But the directness of the comment, coming from this man with the sparkling eyes, was almost unsettling. Sam wondered why Mr. Spencer seemed to take a special interest in him. He didn't know, and eventually he put those thoughts into one of the deep crevices of his mind.

Besides, tomorrow he would be leaving on the journey.

Chapter 2

The Journey Begins

The journeyers barreled down the interstate toward the coast. Although earlier the bus had literally hummed with the excited chatter of the young men and women, it was mostly quiet now. They had been driving almost ten hours, and many drifted asleep, but Sam was too wound up, so he just closed his eyes and pretended.

Kale, the guy sitting next to Sam, came from a neighboring town. Kale couldn't sleep either, so he nudged his new companion, "Hey, you awake?"

"Yeah, I can't sleep."

Kale's voice brimmed with confidence. "I can't believe this day is finally here."

Sam nodded as if in agreement, but wondered how Kale could have so much self-assurance. "Yeah, me too, but I wish I knew more about what's coming."

Kale looked astonished. "You don't know?"

"How would I?" Sam replied.

"Sorry, but I forget that most people aren't from the kind of family I'm from. I mean, both of my parents went on the journey—quite successfully, too. So did my grandparents and their parents as well. We're a huge "journey" family."

Sam tried to hide his intimidation. "Not mine. No one from my family has ever done this before."

"Don't worry," Kale said, nonchalantly glancing around the bus. "I bet most of the others are in the same boat you are. My parents told me to expect that."

"So...what can you tell me?"

Kale shrugged, "Oh, it's going to be awesome. Lots of adventure, lots of new and interesting people...you get the idea."

"Well, yeah, I already figured on that. What else?"

"I can't really tell you everything. I don't want to spoil it for you," Kale said, and then looking around and lowering his voice to a whisper, he added "Look, not everyone is cut out for the journey. Probably most of the people on this bus won't make it. The journey is like a test. It separates the winners from the losers, the deserving from the undeserving. At least that's what my parents said about it."

Sam wondered which group he was in. "Well, I'm ready," he said, trying not to look as undeserving as he suddenly felt.

Sam tried a few more questions, but Kale seemed reluctant to offer much in the way of specifics. Sam didn't say so, but he thought that was sort of odd. He couldn't quite figure Kale out, but luckily the conversation soon ended as Kale finally leaned back into his headrest and nodded off.

With a welcome bit of silence, Sam's thoughts returned to his own parents. Neither of them had taken the journey, so they were rather indifferent to Sam's decision to do so. Actually, to put it bluntly, Sam's father was opposed to it. He told Sam that chasing such fanciful ideas was unrealistic and would lead to nowhere. Why did anyone need a "journey" when life could be lived the way most people did it? Furthermore, Sam's dad liked to say that the virtues of normal daily life and hard work trumped things like adventure and discovery, and there were ample opportunities for education and a career right at home. Besides that, many people thought the journey was mostly a myth.

Sam smiled as he recalled a pivotal scene from several weeks ago. One evening as his dad rambled on for the umpteenth time with his objections to the journey, his mother finally spoke. Despite her own fears for her son, borne from her maternal desire to protect him, she knew that they could not hold him back forever. "Sam must choose for himself," she said. And the decision was thus made. Sam secretly wished that his father understood, and he held out hope that one day he would. In the meantime, their tepid endorsement of the journey only added to his apprehension.

As the long drive continued, Sam observed several others on the bus. One girl had already started a scrapbook. She never slept. Instead she continuously snapped pictures and jotted down notes with multi-colored pens and markers.

Across the aisle from the scrapbook girl, another young lady carefully rested her café latte on top of the new leather satchel handbag she held in her lap. "I'm doing this because I think it will look great on my resumé," she said to the guy seated beside her.

"I don't care about that," he said, pausing to take a drink of the tap water he had brought from home in a bicycle-style water bottle. "I'm not here for myself. I'm here to do my part to fight poverty." He waited for some sort of response, but the girl curled her lips and blew into the tiny hole in the white plastic lid of her drink and then relished a long, satisfying sip. Finally, the young man continued, "Did you know that the vast majority of people live on less than $2 a day? $2! Can you imagine that?" When his seat-mate failed to respond to his question, he just shook his head and returned his attention to his book on fighting poverty. Sam noticed that the book appeared to be brand new, and the guy looked to be about ten pages in.

The combined sound of the engine, the wind, and the occasional clap of the tires created a droning background that was hypnotically soothing. It was the perfect white noise for a bus ride—a meaningless cacophony that nonetheless covered up the discomfort of absolute silence. Out of nowhere, Sam's mind reached down into a hidden crevice and retracted the words Mr. Spencer had spoken the day before. "I just want you to know I'll be praying for you."

"Why did I bring that thought back up?" Sam wondered. He shook his head as if to clear it, like erasing an etch-a-sketch pad, and then eventually drifted to sleep.

* * * * *

The sun perched on the horizon, huge and brilliant in its final moments before tucking in for the night. Three girls sat facing it, their legs stretched in front of them and their hands on the ground behind as they took in the last few rays. They often met on this hill at the edge of their small village. Some days they talked about boys, but increasingly the conversation turned to their future plans.

Jill was the youngest of the three, not an unusual situation for her. Her late summer birthday had presented her parents with the difficult decision of whether to hold their child back a year in school or let her start with kids many months older. But Jill's parents opted for the latter. To make up for the age gap, they drilled her in educational pursuits from an early age; lots of puzzles and quizzes, that sort of thing.

And then there was the genetic factor. Jill's parents were quite simply brilliant. Her dad was the town doctor and her mother a chemist. They took great pride in Jill's intelligence and coaxed her along the path of academic achievement. Praise and hugs were earned in their household, and Jill complied like the perfect child her parents envisioned.

On the very first day of school, Jill met Julie, and they had bonded and remained friends ever since. Julie possessed a freedom and spirit that Jill envied, an easy and much less rigorous approach to life.

Because of Jill's excellence in school, many of her peers looked to her as a leader despite her younger age, but not Julie. Jill seemed to always bend to Julie's wishes when the two of them were together—nothing major, just things like which movie to see or where to go after school. Still, it bothered Jill that she always deferred to her friend.

The third girl, Kristin, had only recently joined their circle. Kristin's family moved to their town from the big city a couple of years ago at a time when Jill and Julie had grown a bit short-tempered with each other. Kristin added a buffer of sorts between them. She also brought a bit of style, convincing them to enroll in dance classes and teaching them about fashion. In fact, Kristin insisted that they all three stay together after graduating and go back to the big city, enrolling in a school of dance.

But today, Jill held a surprise for both of her friends, and her heart pounded in her chest as she nervously broached the subject she had been waiting to bring up.

"I've been thinking that maybe…I may go on the journey," she blurted out.

Any hopes of support were quickly dashed. Kristin spoke first, "Jill, you don't mean that, do you? Nobody goes on the journey anymore!"

Julie added, "Jill, don't say that. You're coming to dance school with us. That's what we've all three dreamed of."

"I'm serious," Jill persisted. "I've always wondered what it would be like to do something different for a change."

Julie laughed, "Yeah, right. I bet you come to your senses soon enough. Besides, what will your parents say?"

"That's a fair question," Jill thought. Her parents stressed logic and scientific method over all else, and something as mystical as the journey would not be easily accepted.

"I don't know," Jill admitted, "but I really am serious about this."

Kristin and Julie just laughed, "OK. Whatever."

* * * * *

The subtle jerk of the bus's wheels rolling to a complete stop woke him. Sam had managed to sleep through the night, and now they were here, just as the sun was clearing the horizon. Rolling his head to relieve the crick in his neck, Sam looked out the window toward the glare of the sun reflecting off the ocean in the distance. He nervously grabbed his backpack, stretched, and shuffled toward the exit door. Kale and a few of the guys were cracking jokes, but an unusual strain to their voices made Sam wonder if they were as anxious as he was.

Once they had all filed out of the bus, they joined up with two other busloads to walk a short distance to a staging area for the journeyers. There were several awkward minutes of standing around, with no one sure what to do next. Finally, a gaunt man with a booming voice stood up on a wooden pallet that served as a makeshift stage and began to speak.

"Young men and women, welcome to the starting point for your journey. You are already among a select group, having made the decision to leave your homes and the comforts you have known to begin what promises to be a great adventure. May you all find what you are looking for." He paused and scanned the crowd before continuing, "Now, I don't want to overwhelm you, but today you will be faced with your very first choice. There are two embarkation points here. One leaves for the flat land. The other departs for the steep land. I cannot tell you which choice to make. That is entirely up to you."

The speaker stopped for a moment to let the words sink in, and then finally concluded, "I wish you great luck and success." And with that, he stepped down from the platform and quickly disappeared through the crowd.

For a moment or two, Sam just stood there staring at the empty stage. No one had told him about this decision. Unsure what to do, he began to listen to the conversations around him.

A young man to his left spoke up, and every head turned in his direction. "I've heard that the steep land is beautiful from a distance, but it's extremely dangerous once you're there."

Another voice chimed in, "Yeah, I've heard that, too. And I've also heard that there's nothing there unless you climb to the top. Talk about danger! One slip and you're dead. The air is thin, and it's hard to breathe."

"And bitterly cold," someone else added.

"I don't know about the rest of you crybabies, but I'm going to the steep land," Kale countered. "Piece of cake! My parents did it and so can I." He looked around hopefully to see if anyone else would join him, and eventually one lone person did—the scrapbook girl.

"I bet we'll get some good photo ops," she said as she marched up beside Kale.

"What's the flat land like?" someone wondered out loud.

An athletic looking guy spoke up and said, "My name's Geo, and I have friends who have been to both places. What you've heard about the steep land is absolutely right. It's beautiful, but it's way too difficult. I'm going to the flat land. I hear there are lots of parties and cool people. The entertainment's great. It's easy to live there and you'll experience things you've never seen or done before. I didn't come on this journey to be alone, and I sure didn't come to risk death or injury."

Kale shot back, "Like I said, my parents..."

"Your parents aren't here," Geo cut him off, sarcastically elongating the word "parents." Several people laughed. "Isn't that part of the reason we came?" Geo continued, looking around at the group, "...to make our own decisions for a change?"

Kale's eyes landed on Sam. "Sam, are you with me?" he asked hopefully.

"I don't know," Sam responded, somewhat embarrassed to be associated with the guy people were laughing at.

So far, no one besides Kale and Scrapbook Girl had actually moved in the direction of either embarkation point. As the two of them stubbornly turned and set off in the direction of the small boat awaiting the steep-landers, Kale glanced back toward Sam.

For some reason, Sam wanted to join them. He took a step, but his feet seemed like heavy steel plates. In his heart, he knew he wanted to go for it. His pulse raced and his breathing became short and rapid. He again tried to move, but indecisive signals from his brain confused both muscle and mind.

As he stood there, motionless and conflicted, he thought, "This just isn't fair!" He hated being forced to make a critical decision of indeterminate consequences, based on incomplete information. He wished he had more time, but he didn't.

His mind turned to his parents. What would they want him to do? Probably they would want him to go to the flat land. Risk was not high on their priority list. His dad might even want him to choose neither, but instead to simply abandon the journey altogether and return home. At least home presented known choices with fairly predictable consequences.

To Sam's great surprise, he once again found himself thinking about Mr. Spencer. What would he do? Sam was somehow sure that Mr. Spencer would choose the steep land. His sparkling eyes hinted at a life of adventure, and Sam reasoned that their confident glint could be borne only by someone who had experienced danger without yielding to it, someone who had probably faced trial and defeat, but who also knew the taste of victory. In a split second of clarity, Sam realized that's what he wanted, too. He yearned to experience challenges, to find the place where life and achievement hang in the balance, to press past temporary setbacks and find permanent rewards. He wanted to breathe the thin air of the high altitudes, and to look down on the beauty of the mountains and the ocean.

Sam's thoughts were broken by a tap on his shoulder. Geo stood there smiling at him. "My name's Geo," he said, extending his hand.

"Yeah, I heard," Sam replied. "I'm Sam."

"Right. I heard you talking to that guy going to the steep land. Is he a friend of yours or something?"

"No, no," Sam hastily said. "I just met him on the bus on the way down here."

"That's good, because it looked to me like you were thinking about going with him."

"Maybe I will," Sam replied somewhat defensively, turning to look at Kale.

"No, you don't want to do that," Geo said with a hint of urgency and gripping Sam's arm. "Trust me. I've heard all about the steep land, and it's not all it's cracked up to be."

Sam turned back, annoyed by the intrusion. "Let me go, please," he said firmly, twisting his arm away from Geo's grip. Then he asked, with a trace of indecision in his voice, "Why are you telling me this?"

"Look, I'm sorry I grabbed you" Geo quickly apologized. "I just wanted you to know that most people who go to the steep land leave the first chance they get. It's lonely over there, and besides, the really cool people all go to the flat land. You look like a great guy, and, I don't know, I just thought you might like to go with us," Geo said.

"Yeah, well, thanks, but I want a challenge. I think I'm ready for it," Sam replied, his voice betraying his lack of confidence.

"Maybe so," smiled Geo, "but what would it hurt to start off in the flat land, get your bearings, meet people and maybe make some friends, and then go to the steep land?"

"Hmmm. Can you do that?" Sam asked.

"This is your journey, Sam, and you're in control of it. You can do whatever you want, whenever you want," Geo replied.

Sam had to agree that Geo had a point, and he certainly seemed to know a lot more than Sam did. He looked again at Kale, who impatiently spread his arms out, palms upward, and shouted, "Last chance, Sam. Come on, let's go!"

Sam turned back toward Geo, who took a step backward and said to Sam in a calming voice, "I'm really sorry. I'm interfering with your decision. Go ahead and do whatever you want, but we'd love to have you join us."

Hidden scales in Sam's brain weighed the words from the two opposing influences. Their weight stood in equilibrium for several seconds, but then the scales began to tip, slightly at first but rapidly gaining momentum. Why should he let Kale, whom he hardly knew, make such an important decision for him? Geo's idea made more sense to Sam. He reasoned that there would be nothing wrong with starting out with the majority at the flat land, at least for a few days.

At that moment, the café latte girl from the bus approached Geo. "I'm going with you. The flat land sounds perfect to me." The ice had been broken, and suddenly a chorus of voices joined in with "Me, too," and "On to the flat land."

Sensing Sam was on the verge of the same decision, Geo put his arm around his shoulder, and before Sam realized fully what was happening, he found himself surrounded by a swelling tide of people. The surge of their movement was irresistible. Even if he had wanted to break free and run toward the soon departing steep land boat, he could not have done so. The momentum of the crowd swept him along, voluntarily or not, in its direction.

Before he even realized it, Sam was on the huge ship. As it slowly made its way out of the harbor, Sam spotted the now distant boat bound for the steep land. It looked small and lonely, with only a few passengers. Geo and the others had moved to a different spot on the deck leaving Sam alone with his thoughts. Deep in his spirit, he wondered if he was making the right choice. The more he thought about it, the more troubled he became. So he did what he often did when he was nervous or troubled—he walked. Moving counterclockwise around the ship's perimeter, he walked from stern to bow and back again, over and over until he was too tired to walk anymore. Then he went below deck to his small cabin, exhausted yet unable to sleep.

And now, in the middle of the night, in the middle of the ocean, Sam leaned against the rail and silently watched as destiny loomed brighter and closer each minute as the ship steadily steamed toward land.

Chapter 3

The Flat Land

Docking a ship can be a slow, tedious process, especially for someone as excited as Sam. As he watched the dock workers busily secure the moorings, he thought how ironic it is that being a passenger on any mode of transport can be so exhilarating, but once the vessel stops, it's almost unbearable to remain on board. Finally, after what seemed like hours but was probably no more than a few minutes, the passengers received word to disembark. Sam wasn't sure what time it was, but it had to be well past midnight.

As Sam stepped onto the dock, he looked around to take it all in. "This place looks great," he thought, as he made his way forward. The mesmerizing lights infected him with a combination of excitement and urgency. He couldn't wait to discover this new place, and perhaps find what he was seeking on this journey.

Maybe he had made the right decision to come here after all.

Lodging and transportation had been pre-arranged for everyone. The drive to the place where he and the others would be living proceeded uneventfully, but he couldn't help noticing that, despite the late hour, there were hordes of people walking along the wide sidewalks lining the streets.

He finally arrived and checked into his new room. It was nothing fancy, but would definitely be adequate. Besides, he figured he wouldn't be inside very much, not with so much to see and discover in this strange new place. Despite the unfamiliar bed in unusual surroundings, Sam slept hard. While his body rested, his mind continued working, like a factory on a night shift.

He first dreamed that he had followed Kale to the tiny boat bound for the steep land, but halfway to their destination, a storm had blown in suddenly, and he clung precariously to the railings as the boat rocked mercilessly in the swelling ocean. He awoke drenched with sweat, clutching his pillow like a life raft, and wondered if the dream was a sign that he had made the right choice. But when he fell back asleep, the dream continued where it had left off, and he envisioned himself in the steep land, climbing and taking in incredible views and vistas.

When he finally awoke, Sam tightly closed his eyes, rubbing and then reopening them to adjust to the unusual light. He looked outside the window, peering at a grayish haze stretching across the sky.

He knew the sun must be there somewhere, but he couldn't find it.

Sam walked down the hallway and found a cafeteria, where he spotted Geo and a few others. "Welcome to paradise, Sam. What do you think?" grinned an obviously happy Geo.

"I'm not sure yet, but coming in last night got me pumped," replied Sam. "All the lights and so many people out—it's definitely not my home town. I can't wait to get out and explore."

Geo motioned toward the table and said, "Pull up a chair." As Sam sat down, Geo continued, "I really think you're gonna love it here, Sam."

"Hmm. How do you know so much already?" Sam inquired. "You just got here yourself, didn't you?"

Geo nodded his head, "Of course, but I've been asking around, and everyone says it's great."

"So...any ideas of what we should do today?" Sam asked.

Geo shrugged his shoulders and said, "The way I hear it, most of the fun begins after dark, but have a look around if you want. Just try to loosen up a little and don't be so uptight."

"What do you mean?" Sam asked, a bit defensively.

"It's not a big deal, but you just seem a little too anxious. Take it in stride. Relax."

Sam thought of his conflicting dreams when he answered, "You're probably right. I'm glad I came here, but I still wonder if I should have gone to the steep land instead."

Geo quickly replied, "Why don't you just forget about the steep land for awhile? You've chosen wisely, so just try to get comfortable and quit worrying about anything else."

Sam pondered that for a moment. Maybe he *was* too wound up. Geo clearly had done a little research, and he was probably right.

Others joined them as they sat and ate a bland breakfast, engaging in the usual chatter among new acquaintances. Finally, Sam got up, excused himself, and trekked into the city to explore his new surroundings.

* * * * *

Julie absent-mindedly stirred her tea and looked across the table at Kristin. Normally, Jill would have been with them, but they had seen less and less of their third companion after she announced her surprising plans. They were all supposed to be equal in their friendship, but Julie was becoming increasingly annoyed with Kristin—nothing she could even identify…it just didn't feel the same without Jill.

"What's bugging you, Julie?" Kristin asked. "You've been stirring your tea for about five minutes."

"Oh, sorry," Julie said. "I just keep thinking about Jill."

"Jill this. Jill that," Kristin pouted. "Can we talk about something else for a change?"

"OK." Julie put down the spoon and sipped on the tea. After a few more silent sips, she mused, "I wonder when she's leaving."

Kristin rolled her eyes. "I have to go. See ya."

Julie hardly noticed Kristin's departure. "Why does Jill occupy such a huge space in my mind?" thought Julie. Maybe it was that Jill had never gone against Julie's wishes before.

Julie smiled at the unlikelihood of their close friendship. In some ways, they were polar opposites. Jill was an only child, the product of a stable, nuclear family. Jill often complained about how strict her parents were. "Well," Julie thought, "at least Jill's parents care."

Maybe Julie's parents did care, but if so, she hardly felt it. Julie's dad travelled almost all the time, leaving her beleaguered mom to do her best with Julie and her two younger sisters. Julie took advantage, not that she did anything all that bad. Instead, she just pushed the boundaries to the very edge and just beyond. If her mom told her to be home by 11:00, she'd saunter in a few minutes before midnight. If her skill set enabled her to make an A in a class, she'd cruise through the class earning an easy B. Sometimes Julie would push too hard and her mom would threaten to bring it up with dad when he came home, but Julie knew her dad didn't want to spend his precious little time with the children scolding and correcting them.

Jill, on the other hand, usually did things as she was expected to do them. If Julie had to choose one word to describe Jill it would be "measured." Jill carefully thought things through. She had a brilliant math mind; everyone knew that. Julie fondly recalled a joke she had made a year or so ago. "Jill, you're like a vector," Julie had said to Jill. "You know, a line moving in a direction."

"I know what a vector is," Jill replied. "I'm a little surprised you thought of that."

Julie laughed, "I definitely remember the word 'vector.' You wanna know why?"

"Sure," Jill answered curiously.

"Remember when we studied vectors last year in math class?"

"Yeah."

"Do you remember the guy who sat at the desk next to mine?"

Jill closed her eyes to try to remember, and then said quizzically, "Vic?"

"Victor," Julie said. "Get it? He was really cute. I'll never think of the word 'vector' without thinking about Victor. Anyways, you're a vector, always moving toward your goals. I'm sure you'll be a doctor some day, or a professional dancer or something important."

"OK," Jill laughed. "So what are you?"

"I don't know. I'm like a zig-zagging circle thing. I don't think there's a math term for me," Julie giggled.

"Well, how about a dance term instead?" Jill thought for a moment, and then added, "I've got it, Julie! You're a perfect pirouette."

Julie laughed out loud, "That fits! I'm still just going in circles!"

Coming back to the surface of her mind, she finished the last sip of tea and stood up to leave. But, reconsidering, she flagged down the waiter and asked for another so she could dive back down into her deep thoughts.

"Jill, the vector," Julie repeated to herself. But it was so true. Jill filtered all her decisions through a matrix of pros and cons. Left solely up to Jill, the safest and straightest option tended to be the one chosen.

Ah, but that's where Julie fit in the picture. Decisions were rarely left up to Jill. Julie knew how to push all the right buttons to get Jill to agree to whatever she wanted. Julie craved spontaneity, and had little use for time consuming decision-making. Just do it! Consequences? Those could be dealt with later, and more often than not, Julie knew how to talk her way out of the sketchiest of situations.

But suddenly the tables had been turned. Jill had seized the "spontaneity label" for herself by the almost unbelievable decision to go on the journey. The vector had suddenly turned in a whole new direction.

* * * * *

As he wandered the nearby streets to get his bearings, Sam quickly understood the reason for the name of this place. It was literally flat. There were no hills anywhere to be seen. In fact, there were almost no inclines of any sort.

Hardly anyone else was out, but he finally came upon a guy walking slowly about a block ahead. "Hey," Sam shouted to get his attention.

The other guy stopped and turned. His eyes squinted continuously, as if he had just stepped out of a dark building into daylight. "You must be one of the new arrivals," the guy with the squinty eyes offered.

Sam laughed. "I guess it shows, doesn't it?" Then he continued, "I was just wondering where all the people are. I saw tons of them last night."

Squinty Eyes nodded and said, "Yeah, most everyone sleeps the day away, but don't worry. Things will pick up later."

"OK, I guess," Sam shrugged, and then looking around and gesturing with his left hand, he said, "Man, this place really lives up to its name, doesn't it? Definitely flat, I mean."

"More than you even know," Squinty Eyes countered excitedly. "Have you noticed that all the buildings are just one story?"

Sam hadn't even thought of that, but he glanced around and mused, "Huh. I wonder why that is?"

Squinty Eyes responded, "Don't you see? There aren't any stairs to climb." Noticing Sam's puzzled expression, he added, "Who needs hills or stairs or anything else that makes things harder? I think it's cool that someone planned this place to keep everything simple and easy. 'Minimal effort and maximum pleasure' is how I describe it."

Sam just nodded along in an attempt to not look surprised. "How long have you been here?" he inquired.

"I don't know, a few months," Squinty shrugged.

"So, how do you like it?" Sam asked.

Squinty suddenly became very animated. "It's the greatest! There's no way to compare what you'll experience here to anything you've ever done before. Trust me, I think you're gonna love it."

They talked a few more minutes, when Squinty said, "Hey, I don't want to be rude, but I have to be somewhere in five minutes, so…"

"OK, then," Sam said. "I guess I'll see you around."

"Sure thing…maybe later tonight. I can show you around," Squinty replied as he gave a thumbs up and then hurried off.

* * * * *

Geo greeted Squinty Eyes as he rounded the next corner. "Did you meet him?"

"Yeah, he seems like a good kid. Pretty naïve, but I see the potential."

"Let's keep our eyes on him and make sure he has a good time," Geo said.

"No problem. I've got this," Squinty smiled.

"I wouldn't be so sure about that," Geo answered. "He seems to really be focused on the steep land. He's the type of guy who wonders what he might be missing. I don't want him constantly thinking about the steep land or he'll never loosen up enough to enjoy himself," Geo said.

Squinty, still smiling, replied, "Give it a few nights and he'll enjoy himself so much he won't even remember that there was another choice. After all, what's not to like about the flat land?"

* * * * *

Much sooner than Sam expected, the sunlight began to fade—well, at least he assumed there had been sunlight, although the haze made it impossible to actually ever see the sun itself. He wondered what time it was and realized he didn't have a watch. No clocks in sight either.

During the day, he had been mostly alone on the thinly occupied streets, but after darkness fell, a steady stream of people began to emerge, much like the lines of ants pouring out of an ant hill once someone pokes a stick in it. He wandered about amidst the ambling throngs, surrounded but still alone. Making his way back toward his new home, he spotted Geo with Squinty Eyes and a gang of their friends. "Sam, I've been looking for you. Come join us," Geo shouted. Relieved to have some company, Sam crossed over and headed out into his first full night in the flat land.

Looking at Geo and then Squinty, Sam asked, "You guys know each other?"

"Yeah," Geo said. "We've been friends a long time."

"Even before coming to the flat land?"

Geo laughed. "Yeah. Like I said, a *long* time."

Just as Sam was going to ask a follow up question, Squinty interrupted. "Do you guys want to just talk or do you want to have some fun? I say let's go find a party!" He starting moving briskly, and Sam and the others had no choice but to hurry to catch up.

The lights were truly dazzling—bright lights, flashing lights, some white and some colored, arranged in every imaginable shape and size. They sparkled, grabbing Sam's attention almost like a carnival barker beckoning passersby to have a look. What an amazing place to be at night!

Squinty led the way, and they wandered from place to place, each one better than the one before. The parties pulsed with excitement, with seemingly endless supplies of food and beverage just a snap of the fingers away. People laughed and ate and drank. Many danced to a continuous music—well, the "music" really was just a constant, pounding percussion. There were no underlying chords or tones—just the steady rhythm of drums accompanied by – what else? - incredible laser light shows. It was stimulating, and Squinty Eyes introduced Sam to several pretty young ladies. One of them coaxed Sam onto the dance floor, and he danced like he had never danced before. He ate and drank, but he kept craving more, so he continued to eat and drink and dance.

How he ended up in his bed was beyond his memory when he awoke the next afternoon. Only a remnant of daylight remained. He had slept through most of it. Fogginess blanketed his mind, matching the haze that again hovered over the flat land. "Whoa," he thought to himself, "I can't do that every night."

So on the second day, he determined to find out what his job would be and what his schedule would look like. Not knowing who else to ask, he went to his new friend, Squinty Eyes and asked, "So, what are we supposed to do here?"

"Do? What do you mean?" Squinty replied with astonishment.

"Well, surely we have to work or do something to make money," Sam offered.

"Sam, Sam...," Squinty said shaking his head slowly, "this is a different kind of place. Have you noticed what people do here? They party. They relax. There's no work. There's nothing anyone has to do except one thing."

"What's that?" Sam inquired.

"Have fun! You are here to experience pleasure, man. Everything you need will be provided to you. Just party and enjoy the moment," Squinty responded, and then added, "Pretty cool, huh?"

Sam's mind toggled between two emotions. Surely there was more to the journey than this. He had always been an overachiever back at home, and because people frequently underestimated him, he had become quite ambitious and maybe a bit too competitive. So just hanging out and relaxing wasn't his normal mode.

On the other hand, twenty years of trying to impress others and even change their initial perception that he was just average had taken their toll. He was tired, and he realized he welcomed the chance to kick back and enjoy the pleasures of this place...at least for a little while.

So Sam dove into the lifestyle of continuous merriment...not that it was easy at first. To the contrary, the years of setting goals and achieving them made it difficult for him to downshift into a more relaxed gear. But eventually he did, especially with Geo's and Squinty Eyes' determined assistance, and before long, the lure of the night became so strong that their urgings were no longer needed. Sam became more and more nocturnal, sleeping through the short daylight hours and awakening to another night of parties and fun.

And what everyone said was true. There were no worries. "Flat" took on a new meaning as it became a metaphor for everything about this place. There were no struggles, no striving, no effort...just fun and pleasure and comfort.

* * * * *

Mr. Spencer peeled off his shoes and socks. The ache in his knees reminded him of his impending birthday, a landmark one representing yet another decade on the planet.

He didn't want to admit it, but his body told him he was getting older. A birthday with a zero at the end of one's age tends to induce lots of self-evaluation, and as Mr. Spencer rubbed his weary feet, his mind moved tentatively into areas he normally avoided.

What difference had his life made? He liked his job and performed his duties admirably, always gaining the praise of his bosses and co-workers, but his occupation had never really defined who he was. Who was he? When he was younger, he had imagined lots of grandiose things, but life hadn't exactly played out the way he envisioned it. He had lived alone now for many years, a circumstance he could have never foreseen.

Yet in recent years, he had come to realize a sense of connection to certain people through the thing that defined him perhaps better than anything else. Prayer. Mr. Spencer knew that his primary calling in life was to be an intercessor—one who prayed for others.

Most often, the people he prayed for weren't even aware of it, though sometimes they were. Take Sam, for example. Mr. Spencer had not intended to say anything at all to Sam that day in the store, but the "chance" encounter had presented such an unexpected opportunity. He hoped he had done the right thing, but Sam's expression had revealed a certain discomfort. Maybe he shouldn't have said anything.

As Mr. Spencer's mind swirled, it took him in a direction consistent with his mood but contrary to everything he knew to be right. His thoughts slid rapidly down a sloping path, finally coming to a halt at the place he rarely visited—the place where fatigue and doubt converge. Suddenly, he found himself filled with a pervading fear that all his praying meant absolutely nothing. Questions darted out of a dark shadow. "Can you name one specific case where your prayers actually made a difference? Can you name someone who has ever acknowledged your efforts?"

He struggled internally, his mind now as sore as his knees. He knew the answer to both questions, or at least he thought he did. But now, in this mood, the questions hovered over him like a morning fog on a pond.

After another few moments, he stood up and forced his mind to snap out of its darkness, and he proceeded to the next activities in his daily routine. After a quick shower, he poured himself a cup of strong coffee, sat down in his comfortable chair, and did the one thing he knew to do. He began to pray.

* * * * *

Entertainment in the flat land consisted mainly of comedy clubs, where revelers crammed into darkly lit buildings night after night. People wandered from one spot to another, always in search of "the place" for that night. The level of laughter in the clubs increased proportionately as the drinks flowed. The comedians' repertoires relied mostly on crass put-downs of everyone who wasn't into the flat land scene. The folks back home who never embarked on the journey were frequent targets of mockery and laughter. Even those like Sam had once been, the goal-setters and achievers, became the brunt of vile jokes and raucous hilarity. But one group perhaps bore more venomous "humor" than any other—the steep-landers. What fools they were! The mere mention of the steep land drew howls of laughter.

Sam reacted strangely whenever someone spoke of the steep land. He was uncomfortable with the jokes at first, and every mention of the steep land, even a derogatory reference, made him wonder what it would have been like had he made that choice instead of coming here.

So one night he brought up the subject to the person who always seemed to have the answers about the flat land. "Geo, I was just wondering…why is everyone so down on the steep land?"

Geo nodded sympathetically and answered, "Yeah, I guess some people go a little overboard at times, but you have to admit it's funny. Anyway, I don't have any gripes with the steep land *per se*, but most of the steep-landers I've met seem so arrogant. I don't know…it's like they think they have all the right answers and they're better than the rest of us."

Sam thought of Kale, and how he had seemed a bit too smug that day back at the embarkation point. But he also remembered Mr. Spencer, and he couldn't imagine that Mr. Spencer would have come to the flat land. So he said to Geo, "Hmmm. I know at least one man who went to the steep land, and he seems pretty awesome to me."

Geo quickly responded, "Sure, sure. The steep land is fine if that's what you want. I mean, everyone can choose their own way, but that doesn't make it right for someone else." His face reddened slightly, and his voice rose as he added, "…and I really don't like people telling me what I should do or how I should act."

Sam could tell the subject was making Geo angry, so he dropped it. In time, he decided the easiest thing to do was to laugh along with the others. What was the problem with a harmless joke? And anyway, Sam still believed that when his time in the flat land was up, he'd check out the steep land for himself.

Geo proved to be quite a champion of life in the flat land. Somehow everyone knew him, and if people seemed reluctant to get involved in the "scene," Geo befriended them and encouraged them to "relax and enjoy." Those three words became his trademark expression.

He and Sam talked about everything…girls, parties, sports…most of the topics that guys their age discussed. Every now and then, they delved into a more serious matter, like one night when Sam asked, "Geo, what do you see yourself doing with the rest of your life?"

Geo smiled, "Sam, you're such a contradiction. One minute you're totally into today and the next minute you're talking about the rest of your life." Then he continued with a more serious look, "I just think when the time comes, I'll figure it out. Don't you?"

"I don't know," Sam replied. "I hope so, but sometimes I think I need to have a plan or something."

"What kind of plan?"

"I'm not sure. I suppose I want to be somebody special. I don't want to be average or just another guy. I want people to respect me and admire me for the things I've accomplished. Do you understand?"

Geo nodded, "Of course. There's nothing wrong with that. I actually agree with you."

"But how do I do that here? It just seems like things aren't going anywhere."

Geo turned abruptly and in an animated voice replied, "That's where you're wrong, my friend. As you just said, the key to your success will be the ability to impress others, and you can do that here. I'll give you a plan. Try to meet everyone you can. Compare yourself to them, and you'll probably discover that you're better than most, but when you find someone you can't beat, do whatever it takes to impress them. A place like this is a natural breeding ground for meeting key people."

"So, is that why you know so many people here?" Sam asked.

"Of course! Do you actually think I *like* all of these people?" Geo laughed, and then he answered his own question. "Not really, but I want them to like me. You never know who might be your ticket in the future."

"I never thought of that," Sam mused.

"Well, there's a lot of stuff you haven't learned yet, Sam, but trust me, you're one of the sharp ones. I think your future is going to take care of itself."

Sam nodded, "Yeah, I guess it will." Then after a moment or two of silence, he added, "But what if I'm missing something?"

Without hesitation, Geo replied, "Don't tell me you're still thinking about the steep land!"

"Yeah, I guess so."

Geo responded, "Sam, first of all, hardly anyone goes there. If people are the key to your future, why would you put yourself in a position to impress the fewest people possible? And secondly, what if the steep land isn't really all that different from here? What if it's no better than this…or even worse than this? Or how about this—what if a couple of guys in the steep land are having the same but opposite conversation right now, wishing they had come to the flat land?"

Sam had never considered that possibility before. "Hmm," he thought, "maybe Kale is over there wishing he had come here!"

"You know what I think?" Geo smiled. "I think that we're having the time of our lives. So why risk it? Why not stick with a sure thing?"

* * * * *

Jill nervously folded her napkin and sat up a little straighter in her chair. "Mom, Dad," she began, "I have decided not to go to dance school with Julie and Kristin."

"That's marvelous, dear," her mother answered. Her parents had never liked the idea of dance as a choice for study. Instead, they had looked into top-ranked schools for elite students. Nothing would be too costly or too unattainable for their only child. "With your grades and test scores, you'll get some good scholarship offers, I should imagine," mother continued.

Jill took in a deep breath, and then said, "Actually, I think I want to go on the journey." There, she had said it. The bomb was dropped and now she waited for the impact, although she knew her parents would likely restrain any strong display of emotion.

There was a moment of awkward silence before her dad said in a calm tone, "Are you certain, Jill? With your academic skills we were hoping you'd study science or maybe even medicine."

"I know, dad, and it's sweet you'd want me to follow in your footsteps, but I've thought about it a lot, and I really want to try this."

"It's just so...so unexpected, Jill," her mother replied.

"I know. I'm surprised, too, but I feel some sort of calling to the journey."

Her parents shot a quick glance at each other. Neither of them had taken the journey, but this was not the first time they'd heard of it. Jill's uncle (her mother's younger brother, Michael) had taken the journey. That's where he met his wife, and they were married shortly after returning home. They often talked enthusiastically about the journey, recounting memorable and life-changing experiences at family gatherings. In fact, Jill remembered vividly one late night conversation between her mother and her uncle. While Jill pretended to be asleep on the couch, she listened intently as the adults talked.

"I wish you'd at least give it a try. How can you be so dead set against something you've never personally experienced?" Michael began.

"How can you be so irrational? There are some things about the journey that defy common sense," Jill's mom replied.

"Karen, not everything can be measured in a test tube."

"Maybe not, Michael, but I rely on facts, not some unverifiable, emotional quest," Jill's mother, Karen, said.

"It might be good for you to let go of your logic and actually *feel* something for a change," the younger brother smiled.

"Don't patronize me, Michael. I think *you're* the one who needs to grow up and quit chasing after fanciful dreams and mythologies."

Late into the night the two of them had continued their debate. In fact, Jill distinctly remembered that such conversations about the journey had formed a wedge between her parents and her aunt and uncle. The journey always seemed to evoke great passion on both sides, and it wasn't a topic lightly taken up in polite conversation.

Today, however, Jill's parents were surprisingly quiet despite her stunning announcement. Maybe they assumed she would change her mind again, or that this journey was just a "phase" she would go through quickly. Whatever they were thinking, Jill was relieved to have it out in the open.

"I think Kale has already left on the journey," Jill added, speaking of her cousin, the son of the same aunt and uncle. Kale and Jill had always been close. He was nearly a year older, but in the same year in school.

"Yes, he left weeks ago," Jill's mom said. "Your uncle Michael wrote me about it and stated his desire that you consider the journey as well."

"You didn't tell me?" Jill gasped.

"No, I didn't think it was something you'd be interested in."

Jill's pulse rose and her words shot back just a little quicker and louder than she intended, "Gee thanks. I wish you'd let me be involved in my own life!"

"Don't raise your voice to your mother, Jill," her dad scolded softly. But then, somewhat unexpectedly, he added, "Karen, I actually agree with Jill. Maybe we've been too structured. I know I haven't been listening." Glancing over at Jill, he smiled and said, "I'm sorry Jill. I want to be open to your input."

Her mother sighed, "Is your mind made up, Jill?"

"Yes, it is," she answered. "I've already told Julie and Kristin I won't be going to dance school."

"How did they react?" Karen asked.

"They think I'm crazy," Jill said, and then added, "Maybe they're right," and after a brief pause, all three of them began to laugh and the remaining tension was broken.

"Well, I suppose we'll support you in whatever you decide," her mother said. "It's not my first choice for you, but maybe you'll learn something valuable."

"And Jill," Karen added, "don't believe something without logically thinking it through—"

"I know, I know," Jill interrupted. "Logic, scientific reasoning, healthy skepticism. Don't worry. I haven't forgotten what you've taught me."

Jill smiled broadly, knowing this was as close to an endorsement as she could ever hope for.

* * * * *

The following afternoon, a lazy Saturday, Jill's mom left to go shopping and Jill began a first attempt at a list of all the things she needed to do to prepare for the journey. She had only been working a few minutes when her dad appeared in her doorway. "Jill, I'd like to show you something," he said.

Jill followed him to his small study, where he sat down at his mahogany desk and opened the lower right drawer. He reached under a layer of crumpled butcher paper and pulled out a thin, black leather-bound book.

"Where did you get that?" Jill almost gasped with surprise.

"Your uncle Michael gave it to me years ago. I stuck it in this drawer and just forgot about it. I'm not sure why, but for some reason I pulled it out two or three weeks ago."

"Have you read it?" she asked.

"Not all of it. Actually, very little of it," said her dad, "but I can't seem to put it down."

"Does mom know?"

"No, I've been too embarrassed to tell her yet. You know how she feels about this sort of thing."

Jill nodded, "Yeah, I do. So, is this why you didn't object more when I mentioned the journey?"

"Yes, Jill. A month ago, I would have been adamantly opposed to your going. But I find all of this to be—what's the word—refreshing and even exciting."

"Dad, I'm so surprised. And glad," Jill smiled.

"And I'm proud of you, Jill. Somehow, I think you're making the right decision."

* * * * *

Jill plopped down on her bed, face up, staring at the ceiling and trying to digest everything that was happening. She could hardly wait for the next few weeks to go by, especially now that she knew her dad fully supported her.

As far as she knew, she would be the only one from her village making the journey. As intimidating as that might be, she was glad. She was actually looking forward to being on her own, and realized the advantage of embarking without worrying about someone else's preferences and opinions. She wanted to do this for herself—not for Julie, not for Kristin or anyone else. It would be a first for her to answer only to the call in her own heart.

She thought of her cousin, Kale. How long had he been gone already? Would she be going to the same place, and would she find him there?

Her musings were interrupted by a knock on the door.

"Come in," Jill said, and she was surprised when her best friend, Julie, burst into the room, excitedly announcing, "Guess what! I'm going, too. Jill, I'm going with you on the journey!"

Jill sat up on her bed, her face frozen in stunned silence.

"Well, you don't have to be so excited about it," Julie said sarcastically.

"I'm sorry, Julie," Jill finally said, "I—I just don't know what to say."

"Aren't you glad I'm coming with you?" Julie asked.

Jill summoned a broad smile. "Of course I am. That's fantastic!" she replied, doing her best to hide the confusion in her spirit.

* * * * *

With the sameness of the days, time in the flat land marched by with little way of marking its passage. There were no seasons, just the hazy short days, one almost the same as the next. Sam eventually became oblivious to almost everything past and future. It was all about the present

There was never a shortage of revelers. Some unseen revolving door seemed to bring an endless supply of new journeyers. Therefore, he didn't notice that eventually most of the other people became disenchanted and returned to the dock to sail for home, their journey uneventfully and joylessly terminated.

One night, however, that reality struck a chord with Sam when a pair of journeyers named Brent and Haley approached Geo. Their luggage dangled from their sides, and Brent began the conversation: "Geo, we just wanted to say goodbye."

Geo's smile faded, replaced by a scornful look as he retorted, "You're leaving? Where are you going?"

Haley sheepishly stepped forward and said, "We're going back home, but please understand that we hold no ill feelings toward you or this place. It's just...I don't know, we're not happy here...at least not as happy as we were at first."

Brent quickly interrupted, "Mainly, we want to say, 'thank you' for all you've done for us. I'm really glad I came," and then glancing at the girl, he added, "especially since I met Haley here. Who knows, maybe we'll come back."

Geo smiled mockingly, "Well isn't that cute. Look at the lovely couple." He shook his head and then continued, "It's just as well that you leave. You're both losers. You deserve each other."

Sam's face reflected just as much shock as Brent's and Haley's. They clearly weren't expecting this level of venom from the normally good-humored Geo. Geo quickly turned to Sam and Squinty Eyes and said, "Let's go with them to make sure they catch the next boat home."

So the three of them accompanied the embarrassed pair to the dock, where an empty ship had just unloaded all of its passengers. Geo said a few words to the captain and then motioned for Brent and Haley to get onboard. The captain rudely remained in the middle of the narrow gangway, making it difficult for the young couple to get around him with their bags. As they squeezed past, several of the ship's crew choked back laughter.

Geo kept shouting insults even as the ship departed. "You'll never amount to anything," he yelled, and then added, "Don't even think about trying a new journey." Sam stood there with his mouth open, but when he looked over at Squinty, he was surprised to see that his friend's face registered a sly smile.

* * * * *

Jill flopped down on the edge of Julie's bed. "So, are you ready?" she began.

"Absolutely," Julie replied enthusiastically.

"What did Kristin say?" Jill asked.

"She went ballistic. I don't know if she'll ever talk to either one of us again." Julie responded. "I even tried to get her to come with us, but she thinks the journey is for fools."

Jill bit her lip, seizing the opportunity to ask the question that had been on her mind for the last few days. "Julie, I was wondering…What changed your mind about coming with me on the journey?"

"I don't know. It does sound sort of exciting," Julie offered, and then giggling, she added, "Maybe we'll meet some guys. I'm so bored with the guys around here."

"No, seriously, Julie, do you think that's a good enough reason?"

Julie bristled, "Don't get all uppity on me."

"I know. I'm sorry."

"Don't tell Kristin I said this, but I'd rather go with you. She's…well, she's a good friend, but without you it just hasn't been the same lately."

Jill smiled. "I love you both, but thanks for saying that. Look, I'm not saying my reason for going is any better than yours, but I just thought maybe you wanted to come on the journey with me for something deeper than that. I don't know…maybe some spiritual revelation or something."

"Oh, sure, that too," said Julie. Then grabbing a couple of things from her closet, she asked, "What do you think we should wear? I can't imagine what I'm going to pack."

* * * * *

After the incident with Brent and Haley, Sam tried hard to shrug off a gnawing question about Geo. Why had he been so rude? Of course, wasn't everybody slightly messed up? All in all, Geo was a good friend, probably his best friend.

But something else deep inside began to gnaw at Sam. He actually understood why Brent and Haley wanted to leave. While he partied during the night, things were just fine, but each day when he awoke, he felt empty, like something was missing. He finally couldn't suppress his curiosity any longer, so he approached Squinty Eyes.

"What's the deal with Geo? He was totally rude to Brent and Haley, don't you think?"

Squinty seemed surprised by the question. "Well," he stammered, "I just think Geo cares so much about the flat land and wants everyone to enjoy it as much as he does. Maybe he was slightly offended." Then after a moment of silence, he continued, "Sam, *you're* not thinking about leaving are you?"

"Well, yeah, I'll admit I've thought about it."

"You can't be serious. Where else would you go? What would you do?"

"If I knew that, I'd probably be gone already," Sam replied.

Squinty quickly gathered his thoughts. This situation had caught him off guard, and he needed help. "Maybe you should talk to Geo about it."

"Do you think it's OK? I mean, he was pretty vicious with Brent and Haley."

"I know him better than you, Sam, and he really likes you. I think he'll be glad you came to him to talk rather than just suddenly announcing you're leaving," Squinty replied.

So the next day, Sam found Geo and braced himself for the expected verbal lashing. "Geo," he haltingly began, "I've...I've been thinking about leaving."

Geo's face remained calm, and he didn't react as Sam had expected. Instead he said in a relaxed tone, "Sam, I know you, maybe better than you know yourself. I've taken a special interest in you from the moment I met you."

"I know, and I'm not complaining about you or anything like that," Sam quickly responded. "You've been great. It's just...I think I've forgotten why I set out on this journey in the first place."

Geo stared intently at Sam, and then stated, "Sam, you've worked hard to be someone your whole life, haven't you?" Sam's eyes revealed curiosity, but Geo continued, his voice taking on a soothing tenor, "Yes, I know how it was for you. Back home, I bet you had to struggle to gain respect, but here, you're a cut above the others. People are starting to notice."

Sam nodded his head. In the brief interlude in the conversation, Sam's mind flashed back to a scene that still haunted him and perhaps even defined him:

Two feet. Sam could see the scene just like it was yesterday. His school baseball team is locked in the district championship game. Bottom of the last inning, two outs, down by one run with a runner on first base. Sam steps to the plate and digs in. Down to his last strike, he swings. Crack! Sam sends the ball screaming high and deep toward left center field, maybe the best hit of his life. It travels 345 feet and hits an agonizing one foot from the top of the fence. Instead of a game winning home run, he has tied the game with a stand-up double, not a bad consolation prize. But the next batter up is his supposed best friend, Colby, the golden boy, popular and gifted—and arrogant. Colby likes the very first pitch he sees and sends a lazy fly ball to left field, straight down the line. It travels 311 feet—one foot beyond the 310 foot sign on the fence, a game-winning two-run home run for the new district champs. The next day, guess whose name is in bold print in the headlines. And guess whose name is buried in the article, an afterthought to the heroics of Colby. And all because of a cumulative difference of two feet.

Sam knew he should have been happy for the team and glad to have played a role. In fact, he alternated between feeling disappointed he didn't get the glory and feeling guilty that he cared. But he did care, and he was just plain tired of being second fiddle. For once, he wished people would recognize *him*.

Geo startled Sam out of his thoughts when he continued, his eyes staring directly into Sam's. "Do you play chess?" he asked.

"What?" Sam stammered, trying, but unable, to avoid the almost hypnotic gaze of Geo's eyes.

"Chess. Do you know the game?" Geo persisted.

"A little bit," Sam replied.

"OK," Geo continued. "On the chess board there are more pawns than any other piece, right? You've got to have them, and they do play a small role in the game. But usually the pawns are inconsequential. The other pieces, they're the ones that *really* matter. Sam, you and I are the bishops, we're the knights. Look around you...Can't you see it? All the others here are just the pawns, like Brent and Haley, moving around in their tiny, predictable steps. I've invested so much in you, Sam, because I'm a good judge of character, and you're better than the others here. We're the ones controlling things. The flat land is our chessboard, and we can own it!"

Sam's felt his pulse rising, and he envisioned himself hovering over a giant chess board. Geo could sense Sam's thoughts as he pressed his case. "Sam, can I count on you? Are you in?" Geo's words flowed out like lava, consuming all other thoughts in its path.

"Yes!" Sam almost shouted, surprised at the forcefulness of his reply.

So the routine began once again, but Sam now began to view things differently. He sensed that he was revered, even envied, and he liked it. After all, he was one of Geo's closest companions, a member of the "inner circle." In a way, he felt sorry for all the pawns, but he prided himself that he had risen above them. Sam began to feel like he *deserved* adulation, and like an aggressive narcotic, yesterday's "fix" was inadequate. He craved it more and more.

Chapter 4

The New Arrival

O n yet another nondescript night, a ship arrived next to the dock and unloaded its cargo of more new wide-eyed journeyers. They filed slowly onto the awaiting platform, greeted by the mesmerizing sights and sounds of the pulsating nightlife in their new home. Most of them smiled broadly and fought to control their trembling excitement, happy to have finally arrived, and ready to experience the pleasures of this place they had heard so much about.

Jill, however, didn't share their enthusiasm. She had not even wanted to come here. On her first day of the journey, she and Julie filed off their bus and stood among the confused group at the embarkation point. Jill's heart had leapt at the thought of the steep land, but Julie had other ideas. An almost unanimous chorus of voices stating that the flat land was the better choice drowned out Jill's attempts to convince Julie to take the other option. Finally, out of exasperation, Jill said, "Fine, Julie, you just decide and I'll do whatever you want to."

Immediately, Jill regretted what she had said, and she felt trapped by her unintended remark. One thing about Jill was her fierce devotion to her word. Too many times in her young life she had been hurt by others saying one thing and then doing another. She was determined not to do that, but she could only halfheartedly follow Julie onto the flat land boat, and now onto the dock in this mysterious new place.

* * * * *

Sam was restless. He stopped dancing and said, "I'm sorry Laura, I just need some fresh air."

"Lauren," she corrected him, but then she shrugged her shoulders dismissively and turned away to hide her disappointment. Everyone knew Sam, and she had been excited to catch his eye, but he definitely wasn't into her.

The noise level decreased slightly on the sidewalk, but not that much, so Sam started walking aimlessly. Fifteen minutes later, he found himself at the dock. He hadn't been here in a long time, and he certainly didn't plan to be come here tonight. It just happened—one of those "circumstances" that lead to chance encounters. With a boat having just arrived, Sam stared down at the latest crop of newcomers making their way ashore and smiled. How long ago had it been since he himself had arrived? He couldn't even remember. "Oh, well," he thought, "this will be fun watching the new people."

Suddenly, his attention was riveted toward one girl as she stepped cautiously onto the platform. She was absolutely radiant, and he couldn't take his eyes off of her.

* * * * *

As usual, Jill didn't notice the occasional appreciative gazes she attracted. She possessed a quiet beauty. It wasn't the flashy kind that often garners most of the attention in high school. Her's was the type that sometimes flies just under the radar, but then at a five or ten year reunion, people look with astonishment and wonder how they missed it. She was of medium height, with the toned body of a dancer and the tan of one who loves the outdoors.

As they drove to their new lodging, she intently analyzed what she saw. True to what she had been told to expect, bright lights shone everywhere. Most people couldn't take their eyes off of them, but Jill peered into the dark shadows. The ambling throngs provided evidence of activity and excitement, but Jill sensed an underlying restlessness. Something didn't feel right to her, and she determined in her heart to resist the compelling pressure to join in.

What was she even doing here? She knew she should be in the steep land by now, but Julie's decision to accompany her on the journey had somehow cast an all-too-familiar net of inhibition. Jill loved Julie—they had been best friends for many years. When she thought she would be coming alone, she had savored the idea of independence, but with Julie around, Jill always seemed to take a back seat to her. Why did she do that? Why couldn't she just stand up for herself? This internal turmoil had been building inside Jill ever since Julie had burst into her bedroom weeks ago.

For the first few days and nights, Jill made an effort to be a good friend. She tried her best to convey enthusiasm as she and Julie set out in search of the reputed "hot spot" for the evening. Despite her genuine attempt, she simply couldn't enjoy this place, not even the dancing, which was perhaps her greatest passion. She had studied dance since she was a small child, both classical and modern. But what she saw here in the flat land was not so much dance as lurid exhibitionism. It wasn't that Jill didn't know how to have a good time, either. Simply put, the pounding drumbeats and the dark, crowded setting provided no context for real beauty of expression.

One night Julie pulled Jill onto the dance floor. "Come on, Jill," she said. "You're the best dancer I know. Show off some of your moves." Jill smiled and unenthusiastically complied. She danced gracefully, yet without revealing even a fraction of her immense capabilities, like a millionaire shopping at a discount store rather than flashing her wealth for all to see. Still, she noticed someone staring at her. "Who's that guy?" she asked Julie.

Julie looked and excitedly replied, "Don't you know? That's Geo. He's just about the coolest guy here."

Jill stopped dancing and slipped into the crowd. Something about the way Geo was looking at her made her uncomfortable, and despite his apparent popularity, he gave her the creeps.

* * * * *

Julie soaked up the non-stop excitement in the clubs. Night after night she made the circuit, dragging an increasingly reluctant Jill along with her. In fact, Jill was becoming a wet blanket, and Julie was getting tired of it. "Same old, same old," Julie thought, remembering how often she had to coax Jill to have fun while they were growing up together.

One night, Julie's exasperation reached a boiling point. She looked over at Jill, and shaking her head, asked, "Jill, what's wrong with you?"

Jill decided to be honest. "I don't like this place."

Julie replied, "OK. We can go to another club if you want."

"No, Julie, that's not what I mean," Jill countered. "I just don't like the flat land."

Julie's face took on a quizzical look, and she asked, "Well, what don't you like? If you ask me it's pretty great here. It's a lot more fun than home."

Jill studied Julie's face for a moment, then replied, "I'm really sorry, Jules. I just don't like it. None of it. I guess the truth is I really wanted to go to the steep land, and I only came here because of you." Several nearby heads quickly turned to pinpoint the source of these unexpected words.

Julie laughed, but her tone showed exasperation as she said, "Hey, I never said you had to come here. Don't worry about me. I'll be fine, Jill. Maybe you need to just learn to relax and enjoy yourself. Or maybe you should just leave and go to the steep land. Whatever."

Jill didn't feel like arguing, so she just mumbled, "I'm sorry, Julie," as she excused herself. Back in her room, she felt a strange sense of both anxiety and relief. Had Julie's words essentially dismissed Jill from any feeling of abiding obligation? She could hardly imagine doing something for herself without seeking Julie's approval, but she also knew she had to find a way out of this place. Maybe it *would* be OK.

* * * * *

Sam still hadn't met the girl from the dock. He didn't even know who she was. All he knew was that he had to find her. Spotting her at the dock had sparked something inside of him. He couldn't explain it, but all the thoughts of pawns and knights and adulation seemed distant and somehow less important.

He occasionally saw the mystery girl from a distance but never could get close enough to talk to her. Each sighting added to his anticipation. She was pretty, and he especially liked that her attractiveness seemed genuine and natural, not the "manufactured" type that requires expensive fashion or excessive makeup. But that wasn't it. There was something else about her.

Sam began to walk about the town looking for her every evening, and he would find her further and further away from the hub of activity. She seemed like a loner, although on the rare occasions when he came close to her, he could detect warmth and pleasantness in her face. Once, their eyes briefly met and he immediately noticed the same sort of glimmer that he had seen long ago in Mr. Spencer's eyes. The girl smiled at him, and then shyly looked away. He stood there frozen for a moment, watching as she turned and disappeared into the crowd. By the time Sam ran to catch her she was gone.

He asked the people on the street if they had seen her, and if anyone knew who she was. One girl said she thought her name was Jill, but she didn't really know her. She had heard, however, that Jill, if that was her actual name, was not happy in the flat land and often spoke of going to the steep land.

Lying awake in bed later that night, Sam tried to recall her face. He already had been intrigued, and now the mere mention of her interest in the steep land made his heart jump.

* * * * *

Squinty Eyes nervously swallowed and gathered the courage to bring up a topic he had hoped to avoid. "Geo," he began, "I think we have another problem with Sam."

Geo bristled, not bothering to hide his annoyance. "Not again!" he thundered. "Can't I trust you with anything? All you need to do is shadow Sam and keep him from contemplating anything of depth or consequence. Keep him focused on indulging in his meaningless pursuits. What's so hard about that?"

"I'm really sorry, but something's going on. I can't seem to influence Sam as easily lately. It's like there's some sort of interference. I'm not sure what it is, but I'm starting to worry we might lose him."

Geo shook his head angrily. He knew full well that there *was* something else influencing Sam—something unseen, intangible, but a force to be reckoned with. Squinty knew so little about the Enemy's weapons.

"OK," he sighed. "If you're right, we'll find out soon enough. But I always have other strategies."

* * * * *

Most mornings Mr. Spencer looked at the names on a crumpled piece of paper he kept on the table beside his comfortable chair, and he eagerly and fervently lifted them up in prayer. On rare occasions, however, praying for them felt more like hard work.

He kept a journal, and it served two purposes. One benefit was the recording of current thoughts, an accounting of items on his mind and heart. It helped him focus. The second purpose was for days like today, when he felt distant and uncertain of his mission. So, as was his custom, he picked up his journal and turned back through dozens of pages. Reading of prior answered prayers, more than a few of them miraculous, once again energized him for the task.

He came to Sam's name and paused. "I wonder how young Sam is doing?" he thought.

Unknown to Mr. Spencer and despite the numbing effect of the flat land, an unseen seed of great promise had been planted and continued to grow inside Sam's heart. The seed simply would not die, but not because of anything Sam was doing to keep it alive. To the contrary, his lifestyle was in danger of killing it. It remained alive only because of the constant nurturing of the prayers of his faithful, unseen advocate.

* * * * *

With this fragile kernel of hope inside him, Sam could be satisfied by the sameness of this place only for so long. And to hear that this beautiful, mysterious girl shared the same passion for the steep land reminded him of his original desires for the journey.

So the next day he turned to his friend and announced, "Geo, I know you won't approve, but I can't stop thinking about something. I think I'm ready to go to the steep land now...just to see what it's like."

Geo's jaws hardened and he bellowed a humorless laugh. "That's not an option now, Sam. You had your chance but you chose to come here."

"Hey, wait a second. Don't you remember? You said I could come here for awhile and then leave if I wanted," Sam reminded him.

"You can leave all right, but you'd have to go home," Geo replied harshly. "There's no way to get to the steep land from here—if it even exists in the first place."

"No! That's not what you told me!" Sam shouted desperately.

Geo laughed. "I guess you need to learn not to believe everything you hear. You made your choice and you have to live with it." He let the words sink in as Sam's mouth dropped open. "Do you even know how long you've been here? Look at yourself. You're soft now, Sam. Do you actually think you could survive in the mountains? No, my friend, you don't deserve to go, and even if you *could* go, you would no longer be welcome there."

"Why not?"

"You've done things, Sam. Shameful things. Things that demonstrate the kind of person you really are—selfish, manipulative, lustful."

The words wounded Sam, but he fought back. "What happened to: 'Sam, you're better than the rest. You're a knight among pawns'...all that stuff?"

"You're a fool, Sam! Words are cheap, but you're too naïve to know that yet."

Sam's face registered shock at what he was hearing. Was he really trapped here now? Had he stayed too long and done things that disqualified him from entering a better place?

His thoughts were interrupted as Geo handed Sam another drink. "Look, I'm sorry I went off on you like that, Sam. You know the topic of the steep land makes me crazy. I didn't mean that last part. You're a good guy, Sam—the kind of guy we need here in the flat land. I'm just overstating my case because I don't want to see you go."

Sam knew that his best move was to act as if he agreed. He needed to keep a low profile and figure some things out. And most of all, he needed to find Jill.

Sam nodded and grabbed the frosted glass sitting in front of him. Smiling, he said, "Yeah, I know how the steep land makes you crazy. Sorry I brought it up. You're right, Geo. A toast: Relax and enjoy!"

Geo grinned. "Relax and enjoy!"

* * * * *

Jill woke up early the next day with a sense of despair. Julie was not in the room, having stayed out all night yet again. She had barely spoken to Jill since that night at the dance club, other than curt, sarcastic comments designed to make Jill feel guilty. For a change, Jill recognized the attempted manipulation, and she mustered the inner strength to not give in. Instead, her sole endeavor became finding a way out of the flat land, with or without Julie. Her wanderings of the past few days had taken her further and further from the center of town. Today, she decided, she would explore beyond the boundaries.

Her thoughts turned to Kale, her cousin. Where was he? Of course, she realized, he most likely had sailed directly to the steep land. She vowed that she would find him there. But first, she had to somehow escape this place that she despised more and more.

Most mornings, Jill would begin her search unenthusiastically, dreading another dead end. But today she felt differently. She shook with excitement, knowing what she hoped to discover, although she tried valiantly to calm her racing pulse in case she didn't find it. Still, something stirring deep inside gave her hope.

* * * * *

Sam stretched and took a long look around his room. It was shockingly unclean. He began to straighten things up, and then, touching his hand to his face, he realized how badly he needed a shave. If he ever met Jill, he wanted to look his very best, but when he saw himself in the mirror, he gasped. Something about his reflection seemed different. What was it? Then he knew…his eyes! At one time, they held a glimmer of newness and anticipation, but here in this place, their luster had been replaced by a faded weariness, pale and emotionless. He thought of Mr. Spencer and his piercing, sparkling eyes, and he wished he were here. And when he remembered the glimmer in Jill's eyes he even more urgently wanted to find her.

The shave invigorated Sam, and when he looked outside, he realized that he must have woken several hours earlier than usual, so he set out to look for Jill. As he walked, he reflected on his journey. He had left home, he thought, to find adventure and promise. Over time, he had instead settled into the mindset of the flat land. At first, it seemed logical that ease and the complete lack of struggle or danger or defeat represented a vast improvement over the alternative. However, he now realized that the absence of difficulty had the profound effect of robbing Sam of something. What was it?

He strained to search his memory banks, recalling something he had read once about trials being considered as joy. Was the corollary of that true then? Here in the flat land, had the total nonexistence of trial and even effort itself robbed Sam of the possibility of joy?

The brisk pace of Sam's walk rapidly cleared his foggy mind. He had neglected exercise and deep mental reflection for too long. It was good just to be walking and thinking. He noticed for the first time the filth and squalor. How had he missed it before? Of course! The nighttime obscured it. The dazzling lights provided a diversion, a false sense of glamour, but the reality was that the flat land was far from perfect.

Soon something else caught his attention. There wasn't much color anywhere. The buildings were all drab and aging, with no real thought having gone into their aesthetic appeal. The paint surely must have at one time been some brighter color, but any hue had long ago given way, leaving behind what one could only describe as pale.

The further Sam traveled away from the heart of the city the more freedom he felt. Far, far ahead, he thought he saw a glimpse of Jill! His heart pounded as he sped up his pace, and before long, he realized he had walked to the edge of the town. He had never considered what lied beyond, and no one had ever talked about it. He looked toward a vast expanse of barren, featureless land, but off to his right, there was the faint hint of a footpath. It was obvious that very few people had come this way, but Sam kept walking. Soon there were small, scrubby bushes and even a scrawny tree. "Remarkable," thought Sam. It was the first hint of vegetation he had seen in this place.

The path angled back to the left and in the distance, Sam thought he could make out the sea. He began jogging, and then noticed a boat with two occupants heading away from shore. Was one of them Jill? He could only see the back of her head, but when she turned to take one final look at the place she was fleeing, Sam knew it was her. He was still on the path, thirty yards from the shoreline, so he screamed her name as loud as he could, but the boat was now too far away for him to be heard. Had she found a way out of this desolate place, and was she now on her way to the steep land?

Chapter 5

The Path

The sounds of the ocean and wind disappeared into a vacuous silence inside Sam's head. All he could do now was watch as the boat grew smaller. Without even knowing it, he continued walking along the path toward the now empty beach, crushed by the prospect that he had lost the chance to ever meet Jill.

"Where are you going, Sam?" a voice startled him.

He stopped in his tracks. Standing there in front of him was another girl he had never seen before. She looked stunning, with long flowing hair framing her exotic face. Immaculately fitted clothing traced the perfect curves of her slight frame. Her sultry voice, charming and feminine, demanded and received total attention. She was simply irresistible, and she knew it.

"How do you know my name?" Sam asked.

"Oh, I know you, Sam. Everyone knows you," she replied. "My name is Gina, and I've had my eye on you." She walked up to him and took his arm, gently kissing him on the cheek. "Why are you out here? Come with me back to the city."

Sam fumbled for words. "I was just walking, and I was curious where this path goes," he replied.

Gina laughed. "It goes nowhere, my sweet new friend." She squeezed his arm slightly and smiled. "Let's go back."

"But I need to know about..." he hesitated trying to recall the name, "Jill."

"Who, Sam?" Gina smiled.

Sam struggled to recall where he was and why he was there. "Um, I—I was looking for a girl," he stammered.

"That's good, because I was looking for a guy," she said.

He had just met her, but Sam simply couldn't resist her exquisite charms. Her smile held his eyes captive and her touch instantly replaced the stirrings that had bothered him earlier. He forgot all about the path and the glimpse of the sea. He forgot about the journey and his lingering desire to see the steep land. He even forgot about Jill, and he returned to the city with his beautiful new friend.

* * * * *

Squinty Eyes showed up at Sam's place late that afternoon. Sam could tell that he was quite unhappy about something. "What's wrong with you?" Sam asked.

"Someone's gone missing," he muttered.

"Missing? What do you mean?" Sam replied with astonishment.

Squinty stared at Sam intently, as if trying hard to read his face. "You don't know what I'm talking about?" he asked.

Sam strained hard to recall something, but he couldn't quite remember what it was, so he just shook his head and said, "No, not really. Who's missing?"

Squinty's face relaxed as he smiled and replied, "Never mind. It's not a problem." With that, he turned and left just as abruptly as he had arrived.

* * * * *

Sam couldn't wait to find Gina, and when he arrived at the spot they had agreed to meet, there she was, as enticing as before. She greeted him with a kiss, this time not on the cheek but on the lips. He liked it, and he liked it even more when everyone in the room turned to see the guy who was lucky enough to be with Gina.

* * * * *

Jill rested under the warm sun beaming down on the tiny skiff as it skipped effortlessly over the gentle swells of the sea. She marveled that she had not been surprised to find the boat waiting for her at the end of the barely discernible path. What surprised her more was that the captain, a kind, elderly mariner—some might call him ancient—did not speak English. But they communicated anyway. First of all, his eyes radiated joy, and there seemed to be a shared purpose, his boat coming ashore at the precise time she had found the secluded beach.

Surprisingly, Jill felt no fear in joining this stranger in search of an unknown and unseen destination. For one of the first times in her life, Jill was doing something unpredictable. She felt as if she was responding to an unseen calling, and it felt like joy and freedom.

The captain offered her food and drink and then gestured for her to rest on a jury-rigged seat of cushions and spare sail. Then with his hand, he slowly indicated a waving motion, and then using both hands motioned upwards in the shape of a cone. She immediately understood. They would sail until they reached a place with mountains. She smiled and nodded vigorously. They were going to the steep land.

* * * * *

Initially, Gina treated Sam well, showering him with respect and praise. "Sam, you're so wise," she would tell him, or "Sam, you're so handsome." He soaked up the attention. Gina was so stunning, and to be praised by her—well, it was not only a boost to his ego but also a huge affirmation of his worth. For the first time in his life, Sam felt like "the man."

But later the tone began to change, subtly at first. Sam would say something, and Gina would criticize him or correct him in front of the others in their group. He never noticed, but she rarely accepted Sam's suggestions, instead insisting on getting her way. She ruled him, but he was content to accept any conditions as long as he could be with her.

She loved to dance, relishing—almost demanding—the attention directed toward her by virtually everyone in the room. Sam enjoyed watching her, too, but grew increasingly jealous. She often teased him by dancing and flirting with other guys. He didn't like it but was powerless to protest. Gina became the fulcrum of his entire world, and his mind swayed like a see-saw balanced totally under her control.

One night they were at yet another party with several couples when someone asked how they had met. He began to answer, but she quickly interrupted. "We met here in the city. He's so shy I had to ask him to dance with me," she said. Her voice normally hypnotized him, but his mind inexplicably returned to the path where he had actually met her.

Without thinking, he blurted out, "No, that's not it. Remember, we met on the path at the edge of town that leads to the sea." She glared at him with eyes that frightened him. "He's lying," she told the others. "There's nothing out there." Her lips curled into a smile and then she laughed, "Sam, you're such a dreamer!"

That night Gina did not kiss him, but instead stiffly turned and walked away. She called out over her shoulder, "If you go out to that place again, don't bother coming to see me — ever!"

Sam was crushed. He desperately wanted to please Gina, and he certainly didn't like being ridiculed by her. But she had changed. Or had Sam changed?

He couldn't sleep. He tossed and turned in his bed. Had the path been real? Wait! A starburst of logic provided an answer. Gina had told the others that there was no path, but then she had warned Sam to never go to that place again. Her warning had betrayed the truth. The path was real! He had not simply imagined it.

As his heart pounded and his head spun with conflicting emotions, he did something totally unexpected. He got out of the bed and knelt down beside it...and he prayed. He wasn't sure if he believed in God, but he fervently cried out for help. And in his heart he remembered Mr. Spencer's words in the athletic supply store, and he hoped that Mr. Spencer was praying for him at this very moment.

There was silence, but Sam felt like something tangible had happened. He opened his eyes and for the first time in months, he experienced a sense of peace in his soul. He spent a sleepless night in bed, not the sleeplessness borne of anxiety, but the kind that arises from great anticipation. Well before daybreak, he got up and packed his few belongings. He knew his destination today — the path he had discovered. Like a magnetic force, it pulled him irresistibly toward it.

* * * * *

Julie looked around the crowded room, but knew it was futile. Jill was gone. She missed her friend, more than she ever imagined. It had been weeks now, but Julie still replayed their last conversation and bit her lip to keep from crying. Why had she pushed Jill away? She could tell Jill wasn't happy, but rather than talk to her and consider doing what Jill wanted, she, as always, had pressed for her own way.

Julie frowned and rubbed her temples to relieve the building pressure. She looked around the room again. There were so many people here, more her own age in this one room than there had been in her entire village. "I can't let Jill's absence ruin everything," she told herself. She would just have to make some new friends. This was, after all, still her journey, and she should make the best of it.

* * * * *

Sam's walk was brisk and determined, so much so that several people stopped and stared at him. Such purposefulness was virtually nonexistent in the flat land, so people noticed and wondered. A few people followed him for a while, but they could not keep up with his rapid pace, and eventually their curiosity waned, so they returned to the heart of the city.

Sam couldn't get to the edge of town fast enough. Just as dawn appeared, he arrived at the same place where he had first spotted the faint footprints, but now there was a sign planted in the middle of the pathway.

It was a startling orange, easily noticeable in a land otherwise devoid of color, and in bold black print, it proclaimed "Warning. Stay Away." Sam ignored it and continued down the trail. As he approached the same bend in the path where he had met Gina, there stood Geo, arms crossed and glaring at Sam.

"What do you think you're doing?" Geo inquired. "Can't you read the sign? You can't go this way. It's not safe."

Sam slowed down and asked, "How did you find me here?"

Geo laughed. "Sam, I know everything that happens in the flat land. I am the ruler of this place and I am your master. I offered you so much, but you have dishonored me."

"What do you mean? You're not my master!" Sam replied with astonishment.

"Yes, I am the master of the flat land and all who occupy it," said Geo, with the look of a wolf baring its teeth.. "And I strongly suggest that you turn around." Sam's knees weakened, but he continued walking. Geo seemed surprised, unaccustomed to anyone actually standing up to his threats. His voice took on an eerie tone. "You dare to disobey me?"

Sam started to run. He could now clearly see the ocean just ahead, and he could make out the outline of a small boat several hundred yards from shore but steadily making its approach toward the beach. His heart began pounding. "I've seen that boat before," he thought. Straining hard, he retrieved a scene from his memory and began playing it in his mind. "Jill!" he said aloud as he opened his eyes. He hadn't thought of her in so long. Was it possible that she was in the boat that now was rapidly approaching?

He ran faster, barely aware of the increasing vegetation on either side of the pathway. It began to take on more color, a healthy green hue. The trees reached higher, some as tall as his head. The grass weaved in the salty breeze, and an occasional wildflower lent its rare color. The ubiquitous haze still hovered overhead, but was that blue sky in the distance over the sea? He called out, but the boat was still too far away for anyone to hear, and he couldn't yet make out the faces of its passengers.

From behind, he sensed a presence. He turned, and it was Geo, poised for battle. He took a menacing stance, grinning with anticipation, like a veteran boxer measuring a young, lesser-skilled opponent. Geo looked older than Sam remembered, much older, and he had obviously been in many fierce and deadly brawls. He bounced lightly on the balls of his feet as he growled, "I warned you not to come here, Sam. You won't leave without a fight."

Sam was not without skills himself, having taken several years of tae kwon do training. Like most practitioners of the martial arts, he knew the first option was avoidance, but it quickly became apparent that such a choice would not be possible on this day. The rigorous training to get his black belt was about to be tested for the very first time in a real, no-holds-barred struggle.

Geo moved first, taking a step toward Sam. His right foot touched the sand, but it was a clever diversion. He never shifted his weight, instead instantly hopping back about six inches. When Sam saw him move forward, he pivoted slightly. Putting his weight firmly on his right foot, he leaned back and thrust a lightning kick with his left heel aimed at Geo's knee. Its powerful snap stopped one inch short of its target. Somehow, Geo had anticipated Sam's move, and he laughed loudly.

Sam repeatedly tried his best offensive maneuvers, but Geo simply was too quick, as he deftly cut off every attack. It was as if he could predict Sam's moves before Sam had even thought of them. And his sense of distance was precise, always staying one or two inches outside of Sam's striking range. Geo was playing with Sam and enjoying every moment, like a cat toying with a field mouse.

The boat was getting closer, and Geo intensified his attacks. Sam skillfully blocked several blows, clearly surprising his adversary. Geo, like so many others, had underestimated Sam's tenacity. Geo was the superior one, but Sam's defenses repelled just enough of the blows to buy him precious time as the boat steadily progressed toward them.

Realizing he may have misjudged the situation, Geo cursed loudly and swept in with a barrage of punches and kicks that finally found their mark. Sam fell backwards and struggled to his knees, but the madman would not stop. He delivered a sweeping combination kick, spinning around for maximum torque, and landed a solid blow to his pesky opponent's face. As Sam blinked, briny tears mixed with sand and blood. He managed to see through the narrowing slits that remained of his puffy eyes that the boat was now only a few feet from shore.

Sam could make out two figures in the boat, and one of them hastily jumped into the shallow surf and was now running toward them. "Sam, hold on," came an urgent shout. Sam recognized the voice, but in his beaten state, it took him several seconds to process it. Then came an astonished recognition. It was Mr. Spencer!

Mr. Spencer jumped between the two foes, and in a firm voice shouted, "Geo, leave him alone!" Sam blinked rapidly as he looked up. Geo was gone.

"Sam, are you all right?" Mr. Spencer asked, kneeling in the sand beside him.

"Barely. A few more minutes and ...," Sam sputtered. "Mr. Spencer! What...?" Sam couldn't even form words to complete a logical question.

"Sam," began Mr. Spencer, "I was sent here to help you. I've been praying for you, and for some reason I sensed that things were not right. Then one night I just felt in my spirit that you were in serious trouble, and that I needed to come here to find you and help you. We need to leave quickly."

It took two attempts before Sam could stand. "Are you sure you're OK?" Mr. Spencer asked. Sam nodded, and Mr. Spencer turned to assist the captain as he moved the boat closer to shore so that they could help Sam climb aboard.

As Sam hobbled close to the water's edge, an urgent, almost wounded plea came from someone very familiar. "Sam, Sam, wait!" He turned, and there was Gina, more beautiful than ever. Her lips were a bright red, more so than he remembered. Her hair, usually a light brown, had picked up the yellow hue of the daisies growing beside the path. She was ravishing, and Sam fought to control his breathing.

"Oh, Sam, I was so wrong to hurt you last night. Won't you please forgive me?" she pleaded. "Come back with me and I promise we'll be happy."

Sam stopped in his tracks, his mind wavering with confusion. She walked toward him, completely ignoring Mr. Spencer. As she glided slowly around him, her left hand trailed delicately across his shoulders. "Sam, it would be such a shame if you left me here," she pouted. Her words flowed with an intoxicating stupor, like thick honey weaving its way into the folds of his brain. He heard the whisper and felt her breath as she leaned close to his face. "Please stay, Sam."

Sam forgot where he was. He forgot about his throbbing wounds. Her honey-words dripped deeper into his mind. All he could think of was her—her face, her fragrance, the warmth of her fingers on his shoulders. Yes, he could stay here with her and be happy. He knew that. How foolish he had been to ever think of leaving her.

A firm hand gripped Sam's right elbow. "Come, let's leave," Mr. Spencer intoned. "Now!"

"Who is this?" hissed Gina, her face contorting into the angry wolf-smile Sam had seen in Geo just a few minutes before.

"I'm Sam's friend, and I'm here to take him from this place. You have no hold on him. Let him go, Geo!" demanded Mr. Spencer.

Sam was confused. "Geo? Why did you say Geo?" But when he looked up it was no longer the beautiful Gina that he saw, but Geo himself. Sam coughed and sputtered with a repulsive heave, his body crumbling. He was suddenly aware again of the wounds Geo had inflicted. Ugly, terrible words and accusations began to spew out of Geo's mouth with volcanic rapidity. The stench of decay filled the air, and Sam was struck with an awful fear, like a weight crushing him down, down, down. His body slackened and he fell.

"Sam, you need to trust me," pleaded Mr. Spencer. "Geo is a liar and a master of disguise. Gina and Geo are one and the same, both the embodiment of evil. He wants to trap you here, but your calling is to something much higher than this place."

Sam was confused and shaken. The short distance to the boat seemed eternal. It took all of Mr. Spencer's energy to lift him up. Putting his arm around Sam, he helped him stagger toward the water.

Geo rushed toward them, and Mr. Spencer held up his right hand and shouted, "Get back in the name of…" but he was unable to complete the sentence. Geo raised his hands to cover his ears and let loose an anguished cry, "No! No! Do not say that name! Be gone, both of you!" As Geo backed away, he menacingly uttered, "It's not over."

Mr. Spencer leaned down over Sam, and said to him, "Ahhh, but Sam, the true Master has declared, *"It is finished!"*

When Sam looked up, Geo was gone. A violent breeze swept past, taking with it the foul odor. Then everything became still and Sam was aware of the fragrance of the sea. A few seconds later, he climbed into the boat with the aid of Mr. Spencer and the captain. The small vessel strained against the incoming waves until it emerged past the break. Soon, the lingering haze gave way to a sun drenched sky, and its warmth touched down on Sam, penetrating right through his clothing to soothe the ache of his wounds.

Sam was fighting a losing battle to stay conscious, but before he fell asleep, he looked up at Mr. Spencer and asked, "Where are we going?"

"The steep land, Sam," Mr. Spencer smiled. "The steep land."

Chapter 6

The Ascent Begins

A few white clouds formed ripples across an otherwise blue canvas. Sam's eyes opened, and for a minute, he couldn't process what he was seeing. Finally, he remembered he was at sea, safely removed from the flat land. The sight of a bright sun brought back memories, and hopes, that had long ago faded.

Sam and Mr. Spencer talked for a long time. With some embarrassment, Sam recounted how he had wanted to go to the steep land but had gotten swept up by Geo's deceit. Mr. Spencer nodded knowingly. "Sam, I once took this journey, and your story reminds me a lot of mine."

"But I've done some things I'm really ashamed of," Sam said. He looked down at his reflection in the water, and what he saw startled him. "My eyes... they...they look so stale. It's like they carry the stain of all the things I've done, who I've become."

Mr. Spencer gently responded, "Your time in the flat land has clouded your eyes, Sam, but there is someone who can restore them to what they were before. In the steep land, you will likely meet him."

Sam's eyebrows lifted, and he quickly asked, "What's he like, and how will I know when I've met him?"

Mr. Spencer chuckled and replied, "Oh, you'll know. He's like no other. Wise but approachable, kingly yet humble. I met him, and it changed me forever."

Sam remained quiet for a moment before asking, "What's the mountain like? Do you think I can climb it?"

"It's majestic, incredible...and every other superlative adjective you can think of. Climbing it is extremely demanding, but if you persevere I'm confident you can reach the summit," smiled Mr. Spencer.

"Have you ever gone back?" asked Sam.

Mr. Spencer nodded as he replied, "Yes, I've been back several times. Sometimes I need to be reminded of the reality and beauty of it. But even though I love the steep land, I feel like my real duty is to return home and bring a touch of its majesty back where I live."

Sam thought about that for a second, then asked, "Then you won't be coming with me?"

"No, Sam," replied the older man. "This is your journey, not mine. I'm just honored to have been offered the chance to help you and point you back in the right direction."

They sailed along in silence after that, watching as the steep land came into view, a vast series of ragged cones rising up from the ocean. They sailed into a harbor, and the captain skillfully moved the small skiff next to a lonely platform. Sam made the short skip onto the dock. Though no one greeted him, he felt a welcoming presence nonetheless.

Mr. Spencer stood slowly in the small craft, being careful not to shift his weight too suddenly. He extended his hand. "Good luck, Sam. I'm glad you're finally here."

"Thanks to you," said Sam, followed by "Hey, what do I do now?" as he shot a quick glance over his shoulder.

"Follow the path, and climb, Sam. Follow and climb." Then Mr. Spencer added, "And, Sam, I just want you to know..."

Sam grinned as he cut off his words, "Yeah, I know. You'll be praying for me."

The unlikely friends shook hands and held their grip for a few moments. Then, silently, Mr. Spencer took his seat as the captain maneuvered the boat away from shore. Sam watched them disappear, realizing that for the first time, he was alone on the journey. He didn't mind either, except for the fact that he hoped he could somehow find Jill.

* * * * *

Geo paced impatiently as his minions slowly filed into the room. No one looked him in the eye, knowing that his mood was pure rage.

"We've lost two people recently, and I will not tolerate losing any more!" he thundered. "Is that clear?" Everyone murmured their understanding.

"OK," he continued, "is there anyone else we need to watch?"

"What about the other girl—Julie?" asked Squinty Eyes. "She was friends with the first one who got away—Jill."

"Yes, I want us to pay special attention to her. We can't risk her trying to find her old friend and leaving," Geo said. "What information do we know about her that might be of value to us?"

At first no one spoke, but then another guy said hesitantly, "Well, I've noticed she likes the clubs."

"Yeah," someone else chimed in, "and she sometimes drinks too much."

But Geo shook his head. "That's not what I'm looking for here. Come on, think harder."

A few moments of awkward silence ensued, then a girl in impossibly high heels spoke up. "She really wants to be loved."

Geo's eyes lasered in on the girl in the high heels. "Go on."

High Heels continued, "That's why she goes to the clubs all the time. She's lonely, and she desperately wants someone to love her."

Geo's voice rose with excitement, "Yes. Yes. That's the type of thing we can use. The rest of you need to learn this. We cannot create—only our enemy, the One Whose Name Must Not Be Spoken, can create. So what can we do? We can imitate." He paused, then looked around the room and asked, "Do you understand this?"

"Not really" said Squinty Eyes.

Looking at High Heels, Geo said, "Help him out."

"OK, " she said, "I think what Geo means is that we find out what someone wants and then offer them a cheap imitation, something close to what they desire, but not the real thing. For Julie, we could offer her attention, infatuation, lust—whatever it takes to keep her from her real desire for love."

"Excellent!" enthused Geo. "Get her to want men's attention so badly that she'll violate her own values. We can start with something subtle, like teaching her to dress more provocatively. Then we'll add something else, like having her talk and flirt and dance in ways that she knows will arouse the guys. Soon, she'll be doing anything it takes to attract men. We don't want her to find real love. If she does, we might lose her, too."

Squinty Eyes raised his hand, "What do we do about Sam and Jill?"

Geo's jaw hardened as he replied, "I still haven't given up. Even in the steep land, I have my ways. Watch and learn."

* * * * *

Sam rested near the dock for the first few days, allowing his wounds to heal. He swam in the warm, salty waters to gently soothe his bruises. He took walks along the beach to stretch his muscles. He soon began jogging and doing push ups and other calisthenics to slowly build back his lung capacity in preparation for the thin air of the highlands above. Geo had directed mostly lies at Sam to discourage him from coming here, but one thing he had said was partially true. Sam was softer now than he had been when he originally set out on the journey. He needed his strength for the difficult days of climbing to come.

Every day he thought of Jill. Geo, disguised as Gina, had unsuccessfully tried to erase his memory of Jill, but now that he was in the steep land, his mind grew stronger and clearer. He wondered what it would be like to finally meet her, and he spent many hours imagining that moment. He also dreaded the encounter. Would Jill remember seeing him in the flat land, and would she keep her distance, knowing that Sam had spent many months in the place she apparently detested? Unable to answer that question, he finally looked up toward the imposing ascent and decided he was ready, so he pulled a cap tightly over his head, adjusted his backpack, and began the lonely trudge.

He walked upright at first, but as the angle of the slope increased, he slightly arched his body forward in counterbalance to the mountain. The path was straight only for a few hundred yards, then it began a series of switchbacks. Rocks and boulders cluttered the trail, many of them overgrown with moss and weeds, making it clear that very few had come this way.

His lungs lapped up the fresh air. He breathed deeply from the pure mountain atmosphere, exhaling the remnants of stagnant, polluted air that still resided deep in the folds of his lungs. He walked for hours, realizing that, unlike the flat land, the daylight lingered past the afternoon and into the early evening, and the sky hovered brilliant and clear.

The tallest trees stretched up over one hundred feet high, featuring a smooth whitish bark punctuated with occasional black palm-sized patches. The leaves, a brilliant combination of fiery reds and oranges, struggled in vain to maintain their grip on the supporting branches. Sam felt as if he were in some enchanted place as hundreds of them silently descended all around him. The array of hues was a welcome sight to someone who had been in a place as colorless as the flat land. Underneath the canopy, a variety of smaller fern-like plants provided splashes of bright green, while smaller bushes added their brilliant red berries.

Even the rocks and boulders possessed far more character and color than the barren, gray-brown dirt of the flat land. Sam avoided the loose stones, but many of the larger ones provided good footing. In addition, some of the roots of the large trees ran parallel to the ground, creating almost the effect of a series of steps, making the climbing fairly easy.

Sam continued along the trail for two days, when toward dusk of the second afternoon, he emerged into a small meadow in what could still be called the foothills, where he spotted a crude shelter. He walked toward it, curious. Reaching the entrance, he peered inside and called out, "Hey, anyone there?"

Someone sat up and peered at him for several moments. "Sam?" came the reply. "Is that you?"

Out crawled Kale. Sam was surprised to see him. "Kale?"

"Sam, it's great to see you, man." Kale responded. Then, with puzzlement on his face, he said, "Hey, I thought you went to the flat land."

"I did. It's a long story, but I finally came to my senses."

"You'll love it here, it's great," Kale offered.

Sam shook his head in confusion. "But you've been here so much longer than me, Kale. Why are you still so far from the top?"

Kale bristled, "What's wrong with this meadow? I like it here."

"I didn't mean to be critical or anything. I was just wondering."

"Are you going further?" Kale asked.

"Yeah, I think so. I definitely want to go higher; hopefully all the way to the top. But you seemed so confident and determined to make it to the summit yourself," Sam reminded him.

"Yeah, I know, but it's..." Kale's shoulders slumped and his voice trailed off, "I tried, but there was a section I couldn't climb. Or at least I don't think I can climb it. It's really tough further up, and what if I fall? I don't know why, but I just lost my confidence and my momentum."

"How will you know you can't do it if you don't try?" Sam countered. "Surely you didn't come all the way to the steep land just to remain in this meadow! Come with me!" he pleaded.

Very quickly, the sun ducked behind the mountain, and the temperature plunged noticeably, so the two young men began building a campfire. Once the flames reached high enough to throw off a welcome heat, they sat down and extended their hands toward the fire. Above them the stars and moon began their nightly display, casting a magnificent carpet of light on the meadow surface.

Sam decided to prod a little further into Kale's story. "How can you say you're afraid of failing? You were much stronger than me that day when you chose to come here instead of the flat land. I wish I had joined you then."

Kale plucked a long spear of grass and chewed on it a few moments before responding. "My parents made the journey sound so easy. They talked about it all the time and everyone, including me, assumed I'd follow in their footsteps. But when I got here, I guess I panicked. What if I can't do it? What if I disappoint them? So I figured I should just stay here. I'm comfortable here, and I'm good at camping. No one back home has to know, do they?"

"You'll know," Sam said gently.

Kale turned away from the fire in hopes that Sam wouldn't notice the tears forming in his eyes. Then he replied, "I've had to work hard to survive. I built this shelter, and I've learned to fish and hunt and gather enough to eat. Not everyone could do that, so at least give me credit for that. I like it here and this is a good place for me."

"But why settle for good when something greater could be out there?" Sam finally asked.

"I don't know," sighed Kale. "I guess I just don't want to try something that I might fail at. Maybe I'm not as strong as my parents. Sometimes it's just easier to accept what you have than to risk it for something you want."

"What happened to the guy on the bus who said the journey separates the deserving from the undeserving? Where's that guy?"

Kale laughed hollowly. "Maybe I'm undeserving. Or maybe I'm just meant to stay here in the meadow. What's the big deal about climbing higher anyway?"

Sam looked at Kale with newly formed sympathy. On the bus, he had first judged Kale to be brash and arrogant, but now he saw before him someone conflicted, almost broken. Sam reached across the flames and, placing his hand on Kale's slumping shoulder, quietly said, "All I know is I'm going to try. I'm not sure I'll make it, especially if it was too hard for *you*, but I wish you'd go with me."

The conversation eventually waned, and Sam made camp in the meadow and spent a glorious evening enjoying the spectacular beauty of the nighttime sky. The next morning, Kale emerged from his hut much less somber than he had been the night before, and he cheerily suggested, "Let me show you where I sometimes catch fish."

But Sam smiled and shook his head. "No, Kale. I've already taken one detour on my journey. This time I'm staying on course. Sorry, friend, but I must be leaving."

Kale nodded his head slowly. "Good luck. You'll need it," he said with a tone of resignation. Then his voice perked up a bit when he added, "And you can always come back here if the going gets too tough."

Sam nodded and said, "I don't plan on that happening. Sure you won't come with me?" Kale shook his head, so Sam waved and said goodbye, then turned and continued up the mountain pathway.

* * * * *

Jill knelt beside the stream and took a look at the gash below her elbow where a tree branch had ripped through her sweater. Dipping a bit of cloth into the water, she carefully dabbed the wound, cleaning away the caked blood. A scab was already forming, an unsightly but welcome shield for the tender skin below.

She wondered if her injury was some sort of karma for leaving Julie back in the flat land. She wasn't really sure about things like karma, although Julie believed in it and talked about it all the time. Julie liked to think of herself as "spiritual," a concept difficult for Jill to grasp. If Jill couldn't diagram something or write it out like a proof or a theorem, she simply dismissed it as silly.

But this journey seemed to be forcing her to reconsider everything. Jill certainly felt more than a tinge of guilt for abandoning Julie, wondering if she had made the right choice to leave. In her heart, she felt that she had. Wasn't the arrival of the boat to carry her away from the flat land too improbable to be written off as a mere coincidence? Logically, it seemed to Jill that it could only be explained as some sort of destiny, and therefore she was clearly acting properly to leave, with or without Julie.

Still, the thought of disappointing someone else had always been difficult for Jill, and she wondered if their friendship would survive the separate paths of their respective journeys. She allowed herself to think so deeply she lost awareness of her surroundings, but the sensation of water touching her ankles jolted her to reality. The stream was rising fast, and she needed to cross it quickly before it became impassable.

* * * * *

Sam hiked for an hour, and wondered why Kale had considered it too difficult, but soon he stood face to face with the challenge that had caused his friend to turn around. At first, it appeared as if the trail had ended in the side of a vertical cliff, but when he finally reached the wall he saw a narrow crack stretching up maybe two hundred feet. "No way," he gasped.

He backtracked. Maybe he missed a turn some-where, he thought, but no, the trail definitely came this way. He sat down at the base of the cliff looming above him and wondered what to do next. Then he surveyed the scene further and thought, "Hmmm, there just might be a way."

He had little technical climbing experience, but he remembered reading something about finding "chim-neys" in the mountain and using them as a means of climbing. Sam looked up again, and the crack in the rock formed a vertical chute going upward. He tested the distance between the two sides of the "chimney," and it provided just enough space to wedge an arm and leg against one wall and the other arm and leg against the other.

He took a deep breath, and then made his decision. He was going to try it! Inching his way upward he covered the first one hundred and thirty feet slowly and carefully. He had hoped to continue in this way to the top, but a new problem presented itself. The chimney narrowed slightly, and then widened above him, much too wide, so he would have to change his technique for the last seventy feet or so.

His legs and knees ached, but there was no turning back. He struggled past the narrowest point, barely squeezing through. Now, the sides were momentarily close enough that he could pivot and stand, or actually crouch, with his feet planted on a narrow ledge on one wall and his hands, shoulder high, on the other. The most treacherous move was the next one. He had to secure his hands and then step across the space between the two opposing rocks, with nothing but air below him. Falling meant severe injury or even death.

Fear paralyzed him. He thought of climbing back down, he was too tired. His muscles began to twitch. He simply could not move, nor could he hold this position much longer.

* * * * *

Back at home, it was evening. Mr. Spencer unfolded the worn sheet of paper and looked at the list of names. He bowed his head and whispered, "Who should I pray for tonight?" When he opened his eyes, they fell on a spot two-thirds of the way down the page. One name stood out—Sam.

* * * * *

Sam lingered there, suspended one hundred and thirty feet up. A chilly gust of downdraft shot through the chute, smacking his face and reawakening his senses. He took a deep breath and gathered his nerves. Searching for a good foothold, his eyes scanned the opposite wall, and he selected a crack several inches wide and a couple of inches deep. His right foot swung across the gap and dug firmly into the crack, and with both hands securely gripped above him, he moved his left foot across. Success! He was now free climbing, and the mountain wall that held him proceeded upward at just enough angle that he thought maybe he could make it.

"Use the legs," he reminded himself, recalling something he had learned from his limited reading on climbing. That technique ensured that he maintained a sense of balance and utilized his powerful lower body to propel himself up the incline. The mistake many climbers make is to try to do too much with their arms. The legs, that's the key. Arms tire much more easily and cannot bear the same weight as the legs.

From a distance, a sheer cliff presents itself as a smooth surface, but a patient climber can find lots of imperfections in the face of the mountain. The cracks and rugged knobs became Sam's lifeline. He would reach up with his right hand and move it back and forth until he found a secure grip. Then he would carefully bring one leg up to another secure place and search for a spot to place his other hand and leg.

Using this technique, Sam crawled upward until he reached another obstacle just a few feet from the top, as the mountain now sloped backward above his head. He certainly had no skill at performing an inverted climb, especially as fatigued as he now was. He stopped and shouted to no one, "Please help me!" The utter silence that met his cry sucked the remaining oxygen from his lungs. Only his panic gave him the strength to hold on longer.

He shouted again, but this time his shout was directed to someone unknown and unseen. His cry originated from the place in his heart where the small seed of belief strained to break through the untilled ground of unbelief. Against all hope, he shouted, hoping to see the one whom Mr. Spencer had spoken of. He looked up, and for a moment he felt pangs of disappointment that no one appeared above him. But this time the sound of his voice triggered a motion to his right as a group of birds scattered from an unseen perch. Instinctively, he moved laterally toward the commotion, making it past an outcropping, and on the other side he found a welcome sight. A lonely tree extended out of the rock and then stretched up to the ledge above him. This was his pathway, and he moved quickly and climbed up its solid limbs the last few feet, until he got a hand, then an elbow, then his arms, his upper torso, and finally his whole body on the plateau. He had done it! He sat near the edge to catch his breath and let his twitching legs and arms rest, and then looked down with wonder at what he had just conquered. In his exhaustion, he never noticed the patch of torn cloth on one of the branches.

After about fifteen minutes, he rose and followed the trail a short distance to a series of stone steps up to a higher ledge. As he climbed the steps, what he saw next was incredible. In the middle of the path, there stood a banquet table filled with fresh fruit, cheeses, bread and meat. A small placard read, "Welcome, all who have journeyed this far. Well done. Enjoy." He ran to the table, sat down and began to eat.

As he feasted and took in the beauty around him, he remembered the food and drink of the flat land. It had never satisfied him like this. He gave thanks for the blessings of this wonderful new place. Then he remembered his friend, Kale. How sad that he was camped just a short distance below, subsisting on much more meager provisions. Sam hoped that Kale would one day gain the strength and courage to make the climb and enjoy the abundance of the banqueting table.

Chapter 7

Sam Meets Bio

A chill greeted Sam the next morning, the kind of cold that makes you slightly uncomfortable but invigorates the senses. Sam welcomed it, both for what it was and what it represented—that he was at a higher altitude now than when he arrived and he was finally making real progress.

He ate again from the table's bounty until he was satisfied, then stuffed his backpack full of a day's provisions and began a pleasant stroll up a forested path. There were small obstacles along the way to keep the hike interesting: a tiny creek to ford, a narrow path circling above a sheer ravine, and even a place or two where he had to actually remove his backpack to squeeze through constricted passages. However, nothing compared in danger and exhaustion to the rigorous chimney climb of the day before. Sam was beginning to think that maybe he had passed the greatest test of this journey. He was stronger now, and he knew it. No challenge could possibly get the best of him.

His favorite time of day in the forest was the early morning, when streaks of sunlight angled down, like golden rivulets weaving through the green canopy. It was still, and the surrounding mountains acted as a megaphone to the sounds of the wild—the birds' excited chirps and the occasional cracking of branches as a larger animal stepped unseen through dense patches. After a solid half day of hiking, he sat down for lunch, aware that many pairs of eyes were curiously following this rare human visitor. Squirrels and chipmunks chattered the news of the journeyer. Once, Sam spotted a deer staring motionless at him for several long seconds before it bounded off hurriedly as if to tell its friends of the intruder's presence.

Later, Sam realized that the company of the animals signaled water nearby. He first heard the stream shortly after resuming his walk. Initially, it was just a white, rushing static, but over the next several minutes it grew louder as the trail began to taper downward into a valley. By the time he saw the river, the roar was intense as water cascaded by, an irresistible force churning down the mountain. The sight and sound of the rushing water was invigorating. Without knowing it, his strides lengthened in symmetry with his heightened senses. Something about a mountain stream does that to a person.

When he finally reached its edge, he realized that perhaps he wasn't finished with challenges after all. The trail led straight to the water and emerged on the other side. At certain times, crossing the stream would have entailed a careful but fairly casual hop, skip and jump. Unfortunately for Sam, this was not one of those times. Instead, the river had widened to about twenty-five feet of sheer torrent. There would be no crossing by foot.

He sat down to try and figure out what to do. The path had been very distinct, and he didn't think he had missed a turn, but he decided to go back and look. While the trek forward had been enjoyable, traveling backward seemed far less pleasant. He had already seen this terrain, so there was no anticipation of new sights to spur him forward. "Oh, well," he thought, "maybe I should just remain at the banquet table until the river returns to its normal flow." Unfortunately, when he arrived back at the plateau, the table was now empty. The reward had apparently been provided on the outbound journey, not for those in retreat. With a bit of disgust for having wasted valuable time and energy backtracking, he trudged back once again toward the rushing river.

* * * * *

High Heels kept watch over her quarry. Julie had fallen into a predictable pattern, coming each night to the crowded bar, always arriving alone, and never really connecting with anyone other than through the mindless banter of the disinterested and the disengaged. High Heels had not yet made her move, but the time would come soon enough.

In the meantime, she peered at Julie with increasing scorn. Why were these humans, these *inferiors*, so blind to their own habits? Why did they gravitate to these dark places in the most vulnerable and dreary moments of their despicable lives? Didn't they know that warmth and sunshine and open air provided an antidote for depression? Ah, but High Heels knew her role, and she took immense pride in performing it well. Keeping her prey trapped in the "fog of war" was made infinitely easier when the victim wasn't even aware of the conflict.

Watching Julie day after day, hour upon hour, presented no obstacle at all for High Heels. Time was not a dimension that concerned her, especially in a land in which time itself seemed irrelevant. Nothing ever changed, except, of course, for the faces.

She often wished she could read Julie's thoughts. Certainly, she could derive some sense of what she was thinking through observation of things like body language, tone of voice, etc., but omniscience wasn't something she possessed. In fact, as far as she knew, no being possessed it, not even Geo. She heard a rumor once that the leader of the Other Side, the One Whose Name Must Not Be Spoken, was indeed all-knowing. But that had to be a myth, didn't it? On the other hand, why did Geo seem so threatened by the mere mention of The Name?

She finally snapped out of her distracted state and refocused. Where was Julie? A split second of panic quickly gave way when she spotted her on the dance floor, mindlessly moving to the music, still not smiling. High Heels heaved a sigh of relief and then grinned. Soon she would introduce herself. In the meantime, she decided to keep her mind off of such forbidden topics.

* * * * *

Arriving again at the water's edge, Sam knelt down and removed his backpack, placing it on the ground beside him. The slight turning motion of this simple action led his eyes to a spot a short ways downstream. There, a tree leaned precariously over the water, part of its roots exposed. He looked at it carefully and estimated that it was just tall enough to stretch across to the other side. Slinging his backpack over his shoulder, he quickly made his way to the tree and began to push. It took a number of attempts, but the roots finally began to creak and then split. Gravity did the rest of the work as the tree fell, making a bridge four feet above the snarling stream, and after a quick inspection to ensure it could hold his weight, he thought, "I can make it!"

Walking across it would be the fastest way, but he was not sure he could keep his balance, so he decided to sit down and scoot his way across. The problem was that there were branches to contend with all along the way. He was able to scoot about eight feet before encountering the first one, a stem stretching up vertically, so, grabbing it with both hands, he pivoted his body and swung his right leg up and around it, back over the trunk. Holding tightly, he then brought his left leg around. Now he was past the branch but facing the wrong direction.

He continued to scoot backwards. Progress was good, until the fabric on one of his pant legs became snared in a thorny vine running alongside the tree trunk. The thorns were stubborn, refusing to release their grip. He leaned over to free himself, but the sudden rush of blood to his head, combined with the visual diversion of the water swirling past, caused him to slip. He clenched his legs against the tree as hard as he could, but it wasn't enough, and the next thing Sam knew, he was fighting the frigid water... and he was losing.

The initial shock sucked the breath from his lungs. Muscles immediately contracted in the cold, making it difficult to react. For a moment, a branch of the fallen tree flashed in front of him, but his desperate reach was a microsecond too late. The water swept him past it, and now he was tumbling like a rag doll at the mercy of the river.

His legs and torso pounded against rocks rendered as slick as oil by the moss accumulated on their surface. He simply couldn't stop. Churning and tumbling, he continued downstream at a speed much faster than he could fathom. He was finally able to get his legs downstream, which helped him ward off some, but not all, of the rocks in his path.

Within two minutes, the sound level intensified to a jet-engine roar. Ahead, he could see a cloud of mist rising dramatically, and he instinctively knew that could mean only one thing—waterfall! In just a few seconds, his body would hurtle over an unseen edge and plummet down, who knew how far...and that could mean serious injury, or even death.

Suddenly, a rope flew past and someone was shouting at him. He had only a split second to grab it. Success! He clutched the rope with both hands as the slack was quickly eaten up, and he felt the wonderful sensation of tension. Only later did he realize how close to death he had come. His legs literally swung out over the ledge, nothing but a spectacular 100 foot plunge below. With enormous strength, the rescuer pulled Sam slowly but steadily out of the raging river.

Once safely out of the water, Sam lay there for several seconds, strenuously sucking in as much air as he lungs would permit. He finally looked up and gathered enough energy to utter a weak, but very sincere, "Thanks."

The man who stood above him was strong, athletic, rugged. He was of indeterminate age, although older than Sam. Then Sam noticed the most amazing feature about him—his eyes. They literally sparkled with a brilliant radiance, a combination of wisdom and fire, warmth and steely resolve. For a fleeting moment, Sam thought of Mr. Spencer, but even his eyes paled in comparison to those that now gazed down at Sam.

"Come with me. Let's get you warmed up by the fire," the man said with both gentleness and authority. They walked a short way back into the woods, where a campfire beckoned invitingly. Sam shivered as he warmed his hands, a blanket now draped around his shoulders.

"I'll be back," said Sam's rescuer. He left and then returned shortly with two mountain trout, which he began to cook over the fire.

"Hello, Sam," the man said. "I'm glad you've come."

Sam was surprised. "How do you know my name?" he asked.

"I am the one who summoned you to this mountain, Sam. We've had our eye on you for a long time."

Sam's face reflected puzzlement, but then showed a hint of understanding. "Are you...?"

He paused, and before he could formulate the question, the man smiled and replied, "I AM."

"What should I call you?" Sam asked.

"I'm known by many names, but for now, you may call me Bio," was the reply. "My father is the one who dwells in the most high place, and he has sent me to bear the flesh of men so that they may know him. I and the father are one."

Sam couldn't contain all of his questions. "But, why am I here?" he asked.

"As for why you are here, Sam, you did not choose me, but I chose you. Long ago, I planted a seed of desire in your heart, a longing that can only be filled by visiting the place where I dwell and where I welcome all who would venture to find me. You haven't always been aware of it, but you have been waiting for this meeting your whole life. I have called you here for a purpose, a purpose that will be revealed to you in the days to come," Bio replied.

Sam thought for a moment. With some reluctance, he finally asked, "But if you called me here, why did I almost die in the river?"

Bio smiled and replied, "Much of what you need to learn can only be understood through trial and hardship. Your first lesson is to trust me and to depend totally on me. Always!"

Sam was intrigued by Bio's eyes. Suddenly, he was struck with a thought. "I bet you know Mr. Spencer."

Bio brightened, "Yes, I've spent time with him on this mountain. And I know that he thinks very highly of you, Sam. He has brought your name before me many times."

Sam lowered his head and murmured, "I suppose you know about the time I spent in the flat land, too."

"Yes, I do," Bio responded. "I know that you made many mistakes and wasted valuable time in that place. I would not have chosen that for you, but I allowed you to go your own way." He peered directly into Sam's eyes and continued, "Be assured of one thing though, Sam. No one has ever come to this mountain with eyes undimmed. Everyone has stumbled on the journey to find me, but I accept all who come, just as they are."

Sam felt deep comfort in these words, but he still had more questions. "And you know Geo?"

Bio responded with authority, "The better question would be, 'does Geo know me?'" Then he added, "He does...and he trembles!"

Sam was embarrassed as he thought about how he had befriended Geo in the flat land. Wanting to change the subject, he asked, "Are you going to help me reach the summit?"

"Sam, many people begin this journey thinking that the goal is to achieve the summit. Your journey includes this mountain, but it does not originate here nor does it end here. The real purpose of the journey is to find me, to spend time with me, and to get to know me. As for this mountain, I will simply say: If you come with me to the steep places, I will show you many remarkable things—things that cannot be learned in the lowly places where the masses dwell."

They continued talking, with Sam asking lots of questions and Bio patiently answering, sometimes laughing, like a parent amused by the way a young child phrases things. The next few days were among the greatest times ever for Sam. They first went back to the rushing stream, and with Bio leading the way, they crossed safely. What had seemed so impossible the day before became quickly achievable with Bio's help.

Sam and Bio hiked together for many days, some-times talking but often in silence, the kind of silence that is comfortable between friends. Bio taught Sam about climbing and scaling new peaks, but it seemed that the lessons learned were not so much about the climbing but about life itself. Sam learned that sometimes the grandest views can only be attained by way of the hardest paths. He learned that some passages were possible only with the help of another. He learned to trust Bio and rely on his guidance.

They became friends, and as Sam progressed in his knowledge and skills, Bio would often ask his opinion or even allow him to take the lead, gently correcting him when he made a mistake or headed off in the wrong direction. Sam grew to love Bio, not just for his teaching but also for his companionship. Life was very good in the steep land. Still, he thought often of Jill. Was she here somewhere in this beautiful place, and would he ever meet her?

Chapter 8

Jill's Progress

J ill was finally making real progress. She had arrived at the steep land some time ago, but the journey often moves at its own pace. She felt a bit agitated and in a hurry without knowing why. The journey seemed to have no time constraints that she could detect. At least she was moving steadily now, and after several days of hiking, she was beginning to gain confidence, still alone, and still totally unaware of Sam and of his hope to find her.

Maybe today, she thought, she would find a new companion to join her in the climb. That would be a nice change. She missed Julie, even though she knew it was for the best that they had split up.

For most of her life, a recurring battle waged warfare in her mind. She yearned to be independent, yet she desperately wanted to please others. Her present situation, thus, felt both exhilarating and frightening. She was glad to be alone and unrestrained by the need to make Julie happy, but she was equally intimidated by the prospect of continuing this journey all by herself.

As she walked along, a sort of ritual began to take shape with her gloves and hat. Upon entering the long swatches of shade that punctuated the path, and immediately noticing the drop in temperature, she would quickly reach into her large coat pockets and pull out her gloves and head covering, the latter of which she carefully pulled down just above eye level and slanted at precisely enough angle to reach the tips of her ear lobes. But after walking this way awhile and then emerging back into the sunlight, the heat quickly built up under the apparel, so off would come the gloves and the hat. All that effort and precision in getting her apparel just right, and yet never totally comfortable—a quite appropriate metaphor for her own life, she thought.

She shook her head occasionally, mentally scolding herself for wasting even just a few days in the flat land. Julie's decision to accompany Jill on the journey had literally stunned her. She wished she had exhibited the strength to go her own way on that first day at the embarkation point, but lifelong habits of not wanting to disappoint others can be hard to break. In fact, she was rather surprised that she had so quickly shown the courage to leave the flat land. Maybe she was finally developing the independence to make decisions that were best for herself.

* * * * *

Julie leaned back from the bar and slowly rolled out the stiffness in her neck. How long had she been sitting here? She was bored, but the thought of leaving to go back to her room almost frightened her. She listened to the droning music and smiled at the girl in the high heels who slipped into the seat beside her.

Oh how she wished Jill was still here. She was jealous of Jill, that she had found the strength to strike out on her own, but in the same instant she tried to suppress a growing anger toward her former best friend. What kind of friend would talk you into going on a journey and then leave you all alone? Of course, she knew that wasn't exactly how the story had played out, but her constant brooding had slowly begun to reshape her memory.

Anyway, maybe it was time for Julie to leave, too. She couldn't imagine mustering enough strength to go looking for Jill—not in the steep land. Maybe when the journey began she could have done it, but not now. She was tired and depressed. No, probably her best move would simply be to return home. She slammed down the final gulp of her drink, as if to strengthen her resolve, then she pushed her chair back and prepared to stand up and leave this hole in the wall for the last time.

But before she stood, the girl beside her turned and, giggling, said, "I think those guys over there are checking us out."

"Who? Where?" Julie asked, surprised at the excitement in her own voice.

"Over there," said High Heels, pointing with her eyes.

Julie followed the direction of High Heel's gaze, and then she looked back at her new companion and smiled. Things were starting to get interesting, she thought. Maybe she should stay just a little longer. Besides, she could always leave later...anytime she wanted.

* * * * *

This place, with its steep precipices and rugged majesty, spoke to Jill's heart, and she allowed the silence to speak to her spirit. The flat land had felt empty, but this place felt different—full, inspiring... even spiritual. Jill pondered that last word. "What does it even mean to be spiritual?" she thought. She didn't really know, but it suddenly seemed important to her.

Lost deep in her thoughts, she almost passed by the side trail without noticing it, but something glinted in the periphery, and she turned instinctively. Rising up perpendicular to the trail she was on was a narrow passageway. Surely she should stick to the main trail, she reminded herself, walking a few paces further. Yet a mysterious voice spoke in her soul saying that it would be all right to venture off for awhile. She had the distinct intuition that the side trail was more than a mere diversion. So, with only a moment or two of deliberation, she changed course and began climbing this new way.

The narrow passageway widened, and for awhile it seemed no different than the previous trail. She questioned her decision and almost turned back, but when she looked to her left, she saw in the distance another journeyer on a parallel path. Perhaps she would find a companion after all!

The girl looked vaguely familiar, probably about the same age as Jill. She walked with the determination of someone out to prove something, "Hmmm," thought Jill, "I wonder if she wants company." She hesitated, but the many days of loneliness prevailed, and Jill decided to try to attract her attention. Just as Jill was about to shout to her, the other girl disappeared behind a large rock. Jill picked up her pace, hoping to have another chance to see this fellow journeyer. Soon, she got her wish. There she was again. Jill shouted, but to no avail.

Despite the gap between them, she could see the other journeyer's face even more clearly this time, and what she saw was both confusing and intriguing. Sometimes the other girl appeared confident and composed, but other times she had the look of a frightened child.

The brief glimpses finally gave way to a longer, uninterrupted view. Jill continued walking, but most of her attention was on the parallel path across the distance. The other girl was walking slowly now, her movements and expressions a fascinating study of inner struggle: confidence versus fear, strength versus weakness, self-reliance versus a need of rescue.

Jill's thoughts turned inward, and she realized her own loneliness. Had her people-pleasing efforts been a masquerade for her desire to experience real unconditional love and companionship? Jill realized, or maybe a better word would be "admitted," for the first time that she longed for someone she could trust totally and without reservation. She desired an intimacy beyond the surface relationships she had so carefully crafted as a means of protecting herself. Jill had rarely revealed to anyone who she really was. Maybe she hadn't even revealed it to herself.

Jill's self-contemplation screeched to a halt by what she now saw on the adjacent trail. The other girl's shoulders hunched further and further forward, and each step was accompanied by wobbling knees. She had no backpack, but it seemed she was carrying some sort of self-imposed burden, and it was becoming too heavy.

That's when Jill saw him. Above the other girl, a strong man with caring eyes came running down the trail toward the girl. "Hold on," Jill whispered quietly, riveted by the scene unfolding on the adjoining trail, like something out of a silent movie. The man was close now, and Jill suspected that he was calling out the girl's name, the movement of his mouth indicating that it was comprised of a single syllable.

Jill's own knees began to waver. "What's wrong with me?" Jill thought, but she still kept her eyes on the action to her left. The other girl had not yet noticed the man running toward her. Giving in to her invisible burden, the girl's body lurched exhaustedly toward the ground, and the man's arms reached out as he made his final sprint toward her. Jill wondered if he would catch her in time, and if the girl was too exhausted to be revived.

At that very moment, Jill felt herself falling, too, and then she felt herself enveloped by strong steady arms. Jill allowed herself to look one last time toward the other trail, but it was no longer there. She adjusted her gaze to the one now holding her.

"Jill," he said, "I've been waiting for you to come here to meet me."

"Where am I?" she asked, suddenly overwhelmed with fatigue and confusion.

"You're on the mountain of mirrors," smiled the man who held her, his face set like flint and radiating warmth and light. "I called you here to see yourself, to really see yourself, as I see you, not as you imagine yourself to be."

"But I thought I was fine," Jill protested. "I didn't know I was so tired..." her voice trailed off.

The man lifted her and then they sat down, knees almost touching, facing one another. "Jill, you've been trying too hard to climb in your own strength. What you have seen is the nature of your need, the need to be loved and affirmed for who you are. You need to cease striving and to rest with me. You need to let go of all this effort you've heaped on yourself, and allow me to bear it with you."

Jill began to cry, a cathartic release, as pent up strands of effort and emotion slowly unraveled in her mind. Finally able to speak, she whispered, "Who are you?"

"I am Bio," he replied.

A moment of silence passed as Jill took in the light that seemed to stream from his eyes. "Can you help me?" she asked, as the reality of his words sunk in.

"Of course, Jill. I always help those who ask," he replied.

Resting there with Bio, she felt waves of emotion—love, acceptance, and comfort. The brightness and purity of his eyes reminded her of her thoughts from earlier on the trail. "Can you help me learn how to be more spiritual?" she asked, and it felt right to ask him that.

"Why do you ask that?"

"I don't know," began Jill. "I've been thinking about it all day. In fact, I've been thinking about it longer than that—ever since I decided to come on the journey."

"What do you think it means to be spiritual, Jill?"

"I really don't know. My uncle Michael probably would say it has a lot to do with this journey. But most of my friends, especially Julie, always talk about karma and being one with the universe—things like that."

"Do you believe in karma?" asked Bio.

"I'm not sure if I do or not," Jill replied, "But I must admit it does seem logical—you know, the idea that the good or bad you do comes back to you."

"Would you like to experience something far greater than karma?" Bio asked.

"What do you mean?" Jill replied curiously.

"Karma represents human reasoning, an attempt to explain things that are hard to understand, but I offer something so contrary and so simple that it is difficult for many to receive it."

"What is it?" Jill asked breathlessly.

"It is called 'grace.'" Bio said.

"Can you explain it to me?" Jill asked.

Bio answered, "When you talk about karma, you are really talking about receiving what you deserve — good or bad. Grace allows you to receive the ultimate reward even though you don't deserve it."

"But that doesn't seem...," Jill waited while her mind searched for the right word... "It doesn't seem fair."

"It is a stumbling block for many," Bio agreed. "Your sense of fairness says that you should get something only if you earn it. But here's what most people miss. Grace is *given* freely, but it is not free. There was a great price to be paid for grace, and I have paid that price in full. I've already borne the punishment for all the wrongs you have done, Jill. That's why I am saying to you, 'stop striving so hard on your own.' Instead receive my gift of grace.'"

As Jill digested those words, Bio paused for a while, and then he continued, "As to your desire to be spiritual, that desire is a response to your greatest need — to know something, or more accurately, *Someone*, greater than yourself. 'Spirituality' is a word that is used too frequently, and often incorrectly. People have come to think of spirituality as something to be awakened or discovered. In reality, that which is truly spiritual is obtained by revelation, not by human effort."

Jill's brow furrowed as the wheels of logic spun in her head. "I don't get it. You're saying that human effort is a bad thing?"

"No, Jill, I'm not saying that. What I am saying is that *human effort by itself* is insufficient."

Jill asked the logical follow-up question, "Then what *is* sufficient?"

Bio smiled, "My grace."

"So we're back to that again," Jill replied.

"Yes, Jill. Everything begins and ends with my grace. Let me give you an example. Did you pursue me today or did I pursue you?"

"I didn't even know you were here," Jill admitted.

"Precisely! I called you, not because you deserved it but because I desired it. Now, think about something else. Don't you find it highly coincidental that your father recently began reading the book your uncle gave him years ago just as you were contemplating coming on the journey?"

"You did that?" Jill gasped.

"Yes, Jill. My hand has been evident in your life for a long time, even if you haven't noticed it."

"So, I don't need to get the credit for anything. You're the one doing the work."

"That's right, Jill. But remember, you don't get the blame either. I took that on your behalf. What's left? Grace!"

Jill nodded slowly, and then she said, "I *do* want your grace. I want it desperately. But can't I do something to repay you?"

"If you begin with grace, why would you ever want to switch to something else?" Bio replied.

"Is there nothing I should do, then?" Jill inquired.

"Simply this—Follow me. I *will* ask you to do things, but you must not rely on your own strength. You will learn to rely on me, even in the areas of your greatest weakness. I am not offended by your weaknesses; in fact, I relish them so that you will know my strength. And you will never be alone in your effort. I will always be working with you and in you. You see, to be spiritual means to receive me and then you will receive the gift of my spirit. Your efforts will matter for my purposes only when my spirit leads you in performing them."

For once, Jill understood something not with her brain, but with her heart. She knew that Bio spoke the truth because she could feel grace and freedom and joy pulsing through her veins. Finally, the only response she could render was, "Bio, I believe you. I trust you. Thank you for meeting me here on this mountain."

Bio smiled. "You're welcome. Now, enter into my rest."

Chapter 9

Sam's Test

T he journey affords many challenges, some of them quite unique, as Sam was about to discover. Three days earlier, Bio had announced to Sam that he would be leaving him to climb alone for awhile. Sam's pulse rose with anticipation. "OK. I'll give it a shot."

As Bio packed his gear and prepared to leave, Sam asked him, "Is there a harder stretch of the climb ahead? Will I be taking on some tall peaks?"

Bio smiled and replied, "Sam, tests come in many forms. Just be careful to follow the path that is clearly laid out on this stretch of the mountain. Remember what you have learned, and above all, remember the time we've spent together."

As Bio trudged off, Sam watched him for quite a while. He hadn't anticipated the loneliness he felt. After all, he had hiked alone on this mountain before. The loneliness quickly gave way to excitement, and for three days now, he had walked alone, but the trail never provided the thrilling, dangerous sections he had anticipated. In a way, he was saddened, because if Bio felt he was ready only for the safest section of the mountain, perhaps he didn't trust him alone on the really difficult climbs. Sam grew restless. He wanted adventure, and he wanted to prove his worthiness.

On the morning of the fourth day, Sam awoke to unexpected voices. When he opened his eyes, he looked up at a gathering of several strangers surrounding him and eyeing him curiously. He was not alarmed by them, but instead was immediately struck by their interesting appearance. They were graying and slightly hunched over, like old men and women, but they had the faces of children. Because of their incessant chattering among themselves, Sam mentally dubbed them "the Talkers."

Sam quickly jumped to his feet, brushed himself off and said, "Hello, I'm Sam."

"Sam, wonderful name, yes, Sam," several of them replied, nodding at Sam and at one another. One of them added, "Sam, tell us what you are doing here."

"Well, I'm on the journey and I've been here for awhile climbing toward the top of this mountain." Sam replied quizzically, wondering why they would be asking such a question.

"Ah, the journey! Yes, indeed, Sam," they chattered back at him. "We support the journey—the quest for knowledge."

Sam's words formed slowly in reply, "Well... aren't you on the journey, too?"

"Yes, yes, of course, young Sam," the leader excitedly replied, "but we were just wondering which path you have chosen."

Sam was dumbfounded by the question. Bio had told him, after all, to "follow the path that is clearly laid out on this stretch of the mountain." He looked around just to make sure, then pointed and said, "Why, I'm following that path, of course. It's the only path there is."

They all erupted in laughter, and one of them exclaimed delightedly, "I told you so!" while another added, "I figured him for one of those."

"One of what?" Sam asked.

"My young Sam," the leader intoned, "you have not yet been enlightened. Don't you know that there are many roads one may take to reach a common destination?"

Sam was confused. "Well, I don't know about roads, but I can tell you there is only one path on this stretch of the mountain, and it's right here in front of you. Don't you see it?"

Some of the Talkers looked over at the path and slowly nodded in agreement, as if deeply pondering Sam's words, while the rest of them shook their heads. What ensued was a lively debate among themselves, which they all seemed to greatly enjoy.

"Sam," the leader finally responded in as wise of a tone as he could muster, "it depends on what you mean by the word 'path.' Certainly a path can be literal, such as the one you have pointed out. But many paths are figurative and more obscure."

Sam paused and then replied, "Well, literal or not, it's not that hard to find this path since it's the only one I see here."

"Ahhh, yes Sam, I understand your perspective," the chief Talker continued. "However, I personally believe that the more literal the path is, the less important its application. Paths that require true enlightenment are the ones that interest me the most. Enlightenment can help us recognize things that the simple cannot see. There are an infinite number of paths as long as the journeyer sincerely believes."

Sam was getting a bit exasperated, and he pointed arbitrarily to his right toward a thicket of gnarly thorns and vines and said, "So you think that's a path?"

One of the Talkers enthusiastically replied, "Excellent choice, Sam. That's the path I was just examining."

Sam could only shake his head, but then he added, "But what if the so-called path you choose doesn't lead up the mountain?"

"Ah, Sam," the chief Talker replied, "it doesn't matter. As long as you sincerely believe you are approaching the summit, that's what counts, and there are many vistas one may achieve. Unfortunately, those who interpret things so literally never find them. You must seek an enlightened status in order to become exceptionally wise in such matters."

Another of the Talkers chimed in, "Yes, yes, well said. And, Sam, answer me this question. If there is a God, or one who we might call the master of enlightenment, wouldn't it be cruel of him to allow only those who choose one path to come to him?"

Sam stumbled for a moment. This was a difficult question. The Talkers leaned forward expectantly, as if they had used this issue often in debates. When he finally spoke, he marveled at the words flowing from his mouth, certain that there was a divine assistance in their formulation. "Well, first of all, I believe there *is* one who dwells in the most high place, and he does in fact desire to meet with us who wear human flesh. It seems to me that your question starts from the wrong assumption."

"What do you mean?" asked the chief Talker.

"You assume there are many paths to him, and thus the question implies that it would be cruel to allow only those who follow one particular way to reach him."

The Talkers nodded their heads in unison, listening intently to what Sam had to say. He continued, "However, what if you assume that at one time there had been no path at all? What if no one, no matter how hard they tried or how sincere they were, could ever be quite good enough to find their way?"

"Go on," the Talkers said excitedly.

"So, in my example, what if there was a time when there was effectively no way to reach God? We could try, but we would always fall short in our quest. In that case, wouldn't it be an act of extreme grace if he intervened and provided a path that led to him, regardless of our own ineptitude and imperfections, thus making possible what had always before been impossible? Yes, it would be just one path, not many, but one path is far superior to no path at all. I would not call this cruel, but would call it great love and mercy."

The Talkers stood there in silence, until the chief spoke up. "Well done, young Sam. Your argument has elements of logical merit—although I'm not saying I agree with it."

Sam's gaze shifted to the lonely peak far above where Bio had said his father dwelt in the most high place. That gave Sam an idea, and he quickly asked them, "Have you met Bio?"

At the mention of the name Bio, they all began excitedly gesturing toward one another and saying, "Yes, Bioism. Excellent philosophy indeed." The chief Talker added, "I've studied Bioism at the Institute for Higher Understanding. It's a wonderful teaching with many excellent tenets. Of course, it is a bit dated. We like to supplement Bio's teachings and make them more relevant to modern culture."

Sam had to restrain himself from shouting out in frustration. He responded, "Bio is a person, not an 'ism.' I asked if you have *met* Bio."

The chief replied, "Of course we all know of Bio. He was a great man, a prophet with many wise words. We admire him greatly and rank him among the enlightened."

"I've met him," Sam said matter-of-factly. "Here on this mountain. And he is the one who can show us the way to his father."

A moment of stunned silence was followed by howls of laughter from the Talkers. "Oh, my young Sam," they said, "You have become delusional, I'm afraid. You must come with us so that you may be enlightened. Bio was an admired philosopher, and Bioism is one of the great, though ultimately flawed, religions."

Sam took several seconds to respond, looking again at the distinct path that stretched ahead, clearly visible for all to see. Finally, he asked them, "How long have you been here?"

"Fine question, fine question," they all nodded in agreement to one another. Then the chief among them said, "We have journeyed here now for many years." The others echoed him, "Yes, many years, many years." The chief Talker resumed, "We are seeking further knowledge and enlightenment from any who pass by this place. When we meet someone as obviously young as yourself, we attempt to share our learning. Some, like you, cannot see the truth of our suppositions, and they regrettably continue up this same path that you are on. In so doing, they miss the opportunity to join us in the real journey of wisdom. There are some, however, who join us in our quest."

"Yes, well said," they all responded. Two or three of them enthusiastically added, "I am one who now seeks the new paths!"

The chief then looked at Sam and asked, "My young friend, Sam, would you like to join us? There are many other interesting philosophies to explore. Don't become constrained by the teachings of Bioism. Join us, and we can share our knowledge of such things with you. You will experience true freedom, and you can journey with us toward true enlightenment."

Sam simply replied, "I don't know much about philosophies and 'isms.' I just know that I've met Bio." Sensing their doubt, he quickly added, "And so has my friend, Mr. Spencer."

At the mention of that name, the Talkers huddled together, whispering and shaking their heads. The chief looked up and said, "Do you refer to Dr. Quinton Spencer of the Dome Theological Institute?"

Sam laughed, "No, it's a different Mr. Spencer."

"We've not heard of this Mr. Spencer. Is he published? Has he achieved some sort of notoriety?" they asked.

"No," Sam replied, "He's just a man I know who has made a difference in my life."

"I see. Very well, then," the Talkers huffed, their body language clearly indicating that the opinion of a common man bore little influence with them. "Perhaps you should summon this Mr. Spencer fellow to join us as well. We merely seek to enlighten the uneducated."

"No thanks," Sam said.

"It was a pleasure to meet you, nonetheless, young Sam" the chief Talker finally said. "Perhaps we'll see you again when we return to these parts."

By now, Sam realized that he would never convince the Talkers of his position, but he also sensed that they could not refute his personal experience. In some ways, the debate concluded in a draw, but as they set off on a "new path" through the rough thicket, with vines and branches clawing at their every movement, Sam was pretty convinced of his own position in the argument. He watched them marching away, and although he had no intention of joining them, he couldn't resist following them for awhile. He chuckled at how they rationalized the existence of a "path" when there was no perceptible trail to follow.

Just as he was about to turn around, he heard something far below. Pulling out a pair of binoculars, he spotted a group huddled next to some rugged outcroppings, posing for pictures. They took endless shots, sometimes with the entire group, sometimes in pairs or other subsets, and even a number of individual shots. They were immaculately dressed, with matching fleece jackets and all the latest outdoor fashions and high-tech gear, everything from designer polarized sunglasses down to expensive water-repellent boots.

After their photo session ended, they sat around a huge fire pit in comfortable camp chairs, the kind that fold up neatly into nylon pouches. Cords of firewood stood conveniently near the fire, row after row stacked in perfectly symmetrical lines. It was obvious that this group had been camped out here for a long time. Their tents provided maximum comfort. They drank hot chocolate from their insulated mugs and laughed as they shared stories by the fire.

One girl looked vaguely familiar. He strained to remember how he knew that face, and then he remembered. It was the girl from the bus, Scrapbook Girl.

Sam continued to watch them. On cue, they all stood up and entered their tents. Fifteen minutes later, they emerged in different clothing, equally impressive in style and quality, but no longer color coordinated. Time for another photo shoot! This time, they took mostly individual action shots to simulate climbing the nearby outcroppings. The second camera session lasted longer than the first since they all took turns climbing a short ways up for the picture and then back down.

When they were satisfied with the results, they sat again by the fire pit, and one of them stood for what appeared to be an instructional session. Sam couldn't see precisely what was being demonstrated, although it seemed to involve ropes and fasteners. As the instructor showed them the various techniques, they all took diligent notes.

Sam eventually tired of watching them, and made his way back to the path. When he arrived, Bio was waiting for him. "Sam, you did well on the test."

Sam shook his head and replied, "You mean that was my test? It didn't feel like one. This section of the trail hasn't been all that difficult to follow — well, for me at least — but I guess I did meet some pretty interesting people. Who were they, anyway?"

Bio answered, "As you may have surmised, the test was not the climb but rather the dialogue with the people you met. I'm glad their words didn't sway you."

Sam responded excitedly, "Yeah, they really do like to debate, don't they. In fact, I gave them a name — the Talkers."

Bio smiled, "That's a good name for them. They love to argue and engage in endless discussions of philosophy. I invited them to this mountain, but they refuse to seek me. Instead, they just wander about in circles, never gaining altitude or understanding. They think they are wise, but their refusal to accept the simplicity of my path reveals their ignorance." And then raising his voice in a way that implied authority rather than anger, he added, "And never let anyone convince you to add to or change my word. It speaks truth to all generations. Listen to me and speak the words I teach you. Nothing else is needed."

Sam nodded slowly, his mind taking its time in deciphering the meaning of Bio's words. "So, do you think my answer was OK when they asked the question about whether it is cruel to allow only one path?"

"Yes," Bio responded approvingly. "My father desires all to come to him, but they must do so by way of the path that I laid—at great cost, I might add."

"What do you mean—great cost?" Sam inquired.

"One day you will see with your own eyes what I mean. There is a place above that could never be crossed except by means of the one way my father provided—a bridge that I laid with my own flesh and blood. The adversary you know as Geo waged a great war with me. He thought he had won by killing me, but in fact he only bruised me." With that statement, Bio removed his shoe and pulled down his sock to reveal a purplish red scar on his heel, and then he added, "If you look carefully, you can still see drops of blood from this wound along the pathway that you now follow."

Sam instinctively looked down, and it took him only a moment to find a crusted reddish stain on one of the rocks along the path. "You left a trail of blood?" he gasped. "That must have been excruciatingly painful."

"Yes, Sam, but it also was joyful. In fact, the joy of knowing you and others could one day follow the path enabled me to endure the pain."

Sam fell to his knees with gratitude. "How can I ever thank you for what you've done?"

"Your presence with me is thanks enough," Bio replied as he extended his hand to lift Sam back to his feet.

"Will the Talkers ever find their way?" Sam asked.

Bio smiled, "The invitation stands. They still may find their way if they choose to follow."

Sam asked, "What about the others down below?"

"I call them the Posers," Bio replied. "They dress in all the right clothing, with just the right technical gear. They love to take pictures, as if they were posing for a photo shoot in an outdoor gear catalog. They attend training clinics for climbers, and they write articles about mountaineering, but they never go anywhere. They never put their clothing or equipment to the real test. They prefer to look the part without engaging in the climb. Always be on your guard for people like these, Sam, because they're very intent on recruiting others to join them."

Sam inquired, "Why do they do this?"

Bio replied, "There is an adversary who is a master at leading men and women astray. You've met him, Sam. Geo is but one of his many names and faces, and he employs many tactics to disrupt the journey. Even those who come to the steep land are not exempt from his attacks."

Sam shivered as the temperature seemed to fall momentarily at the very mention of that name. He wondered if Geo would ever pursue him again, but shook his head vigorously to clear the thought.

Bio continued, "Many other groups besides the Talkers and the Posers have perverted the journey, and even more will spring up in the days to come. The path is distinct, but it is difficult. Few actually follow it, and no one can complete it without hearing my call and following my direction."

Sam took it all in, pleased that he had passed this first test, and also wondering what future tests lay ahead.

Chapter 10

Sam Learns a Lesson

They moved on to higher elevations, and snow began falling, not the gentle flaky stuff, but swirling icy pins pricking Sam's face so hard that he pulled his hood tightly around his head and kept his face pointed downward. He wouldn't have been able to see very far anyways with the visibility reduced to almost nothing by the white swirl. Sam was thus taken by complete surprise when they reached a new and imposing obstacle. A steep mountain face blocked their path. The only way to continue this part of the journey required scaling a sheer wall of thick glacial ice.

"What do we do now?" Sam asked.

Bio replied, "I'll never call you to a task without equipping you to accomplish it. This wall cannot be climbed without the proper shoes and an ice axe." With that, Bio ducked into a small cave opening that Sam had not noticed before. When he emerged, he had with him the climbing equipment that Sam would need.

Bio handed them to Sam and led him around to a much smaller icy face on an adjoining peak. "Sam, we'll train here before we continue the climb." Bio then demonstrated how to dig the shoes and thrust the axe into the ice. He let Sam try it, correcting and helping him. It was hard work, and they remained there together all day, practicing the technique over and over, and trying it on steeper and steeper areas.

"Sam," Bio said, "I want you to stay here and train on this smaller mountain. I must go for awhile. Keep working, and be ready. When the time comes for you to continue your journey, I will summon you."

"You're going to leave me here?" Sam protested. "Why?"

Bio patiently answered, "Sometimes on the journey, you'll be given small things. Once you've mastered them, then I'll give you greater things."

"Well, how long do I have to wait here?" Sam inquired.

"Time is measured differently here, Sam. When I am ready for you to proceed, you will know."

"How will I know?" Sam replied. "Will you come get me?"

"You will know," Bio stated firmly. "For now, I need you to remain here and train diligently. You'll need all your skills when the time comes." And with that, he was gone.

* * * * *

Julie took the tissue from the hand of High Heels and swabbed her moist cheeks. "I wish I could see her and tell her I'm sorry."

"Sorry? Why? You didn't *force* her to leave, did you?" asked High Heels.

"No, but I definitely pushed her away," sobbed Julie.

"You're too hard on yourself, Julie. It sounds to me like Jill wasn't nearly as good of a friend as your memory makes her out to be."

"What do you mean?"

"From what you've told me, you were just wanting Jill to be happy. All you did was to tell her to snap out of her isolation and enjoy herself. But, as they say, misery loves company." High Heels paused for effect, and then continued, "...and it sounds to me like Jill was jealous of you."

"Jealous? Of me?" Julie stammered.

"Sure she was. You're happy. You're beautiful and sexy and fun. Jill is plain and boring, and she wanted you to be just as miserable as she was. Don't you see that?"

"Well, maybe..."

"No maybe about it, Julie. Jill abandoned you, not the other way around. Quit blaming yourself. Jill's a big girl, and if she wants to ruin a great thing and stomp out her deepest friendship, you'll just have to accept it and move on. You're not to blame. Zero percent. The way I see it, it's all on Jill."

Julie stopped crying and straightened up slightly in her chair. Did this make sense? Maybe it did.

"You're still here. Enjoy it, Julie."

Julie's thrust her jaw slightly forward, and the wetness in her eyes gave way to a hard glare. "You're right!" she finally said, looking back at High Heels. "I've been blaming myself for too long. It's time to blame the real culprit—Jill. I hope she's having a rotten time in the steep land, or wherever she is now."

High Heels smiled, "That's the way, Julie." She grasped Julie's hand and held it as if to comfort her, but in a dimension that Julie could not see, her fingers spread out like spiders spinning a web as they curled around their prey.

* * * * *

The meeting was nearing an end. Geo listened approvingly as Squinty Eyes reported on a new arrival he'd befriended, a guy enamored with rigid rule-keeping, and perhaps more significantly, with pointing out the flaws in everyone else.

"We can use that," Geo said.   "OK," he continued as Squinty sat down, "now let's get an update on Julie."

High Heels stood up and began, "Everything is going great. She's taken the bait on making the pursuit of guys her primary goal. You should see the clothes I've convinced her to wear—tight and revealing. The guys definitely notice. Plus, I've been able to add a new wrinkle that I think you'll like."

Geo's eyebrows arched, "What's that?"

"Bitterness," replied High Heels, with more than a little pride in her resourcefulness.

"Ah, I like it! Go on," Geo said.

"Thanks! I had a real battle on my hands. Julie is so blind...stupid really. She totally ignored her friend, Jill, when they first arrived. Jill hated the flat land. She's one of those," High Heels said while making quotation marks with her fingers, and everyone around the room nodded knowingly.

"Anyways," High Heels continued, "Jill left, and Julie blamed herself. I had to work overtime to avoid that. In fact, she was ready to *forgive* Jill."

An audible gasp echoed through the room. High Heels had used the forbidden word. *Forgive*. It was rarely spoken in the flat land; Geo hated this word so much that its use was all but banished. High Heels, realizing her scandalous mistake, cowered down and waited for her punishment.

Geo's fist slammed on the table. "All of you listen to me," Geo hissed. "You've heard a word tonight that does not exist in our domain. Forget this word. It must never be spoken again." He walked over to High Heels and stood over her. "Never! Never!" Do you understand me!?" his voice boomed.

She flattened her body onto the floor and curled up into a fetal position, waiting for more verbal lashing—or even worse. Inexplicably, Geo chose to let the offense go unpunished, and he backed away.

"I will spare you tonight, because you have done well with Julie." Then turning his head from side to side, he addressed the others. "Bitterness is a powerful weapon. It will fester and spread like a cancer, consuming our target's thoughts—robbing her of peace and of healing. If Julie truly embraces her bitterness, we will soon be able to relax our guard and move on to other subjects. Note this when you return to your duties, and you will see our land is filled with such people."

Geo nodded his approval to High Heels, and she gratefully rose to her feet, still shaking but happy to be alive.

* * * * *

Sam poured all his efforts into the training. He climbed and re-climbed the small mountain, perfecting the techniques mandated by the icy conditions. At first, he was patient, content to wait for Bio's call to continue. However, as the days wore on and on, Sam began to tire of waiting and training. One day, as he strained to put on the heavy boots one more time, he threw them down in disgust.

"I'm ready!" he shouted toward the mountain. "Bio, where are you?" He was angry now, furious that Bio was making him wait longer than he thought necessary. "This is just a massive waste of time and talent," he muttered to no one. He yearned to be making progress, and waiting around on Bio was an unproductive waste.

His continued shouts toward the mountain were met with silence. The falling snow provided no sound, either, but one full-mooned night an eerie howl from a lonely wolf pierced the stillness. From behind him came a voice that was all too familiar. "Sam, what are you doing?" He turned to look, although he already knew the source of the words. It was Geo! He looked pale and sickly, his eyes darting back and forth constantly, as if he were fearful and uncomfortable in this high place.

"Geo, what are you doing here?" Sam asked warily.

"Sam, the question is 'what are *you* doing here?'" Geo asked with a face fluctuating between ridicule and concern.

"Bio told me to wait here," Sam replied nervously.

Geo laughed, "Sam, why should you wait? You're ready. You know it. He just wants to limit you and turn you into a puppet that he can control. He doesn't see your true potential like I still do. You don't have to listen to him, Sam." Looking around for dramatic effect, he then inquired, "Where is he, by the way? Has he left you here all alone?"

"He went ahead," Sam admitted, but then rushed to add, "but he said he'll come back to get me."

"Surely he would have come for you by now, Sam," Geo smirked. "Maybe he forgot, or maybe he doesn't trust you. Perhaps he wants you to prove that you're a man. Or are you still just a boy?" At that moment, a thunderclap sounded overhead, rattling loose ice and rocks from above that rained down all around them. Geo's face showed alarm, and suddenly he was gone.

Sam fought to remove Geo from his mind as he shook his head and sat down in the snow. Had the conversation really happened, or was Sam just imagining things, his mind numbed by the high altitude?

He continued to wait, but as the days crept by, he could barely stand the silence. Where was Bio? Finally, he couldn't take it any longer. Bio had somehow forgotten him, so Sam decided he would climb the mountain and find him. He would conquer it on his own, and Bio would be proud of Sam's initiative and bravery. So he clipped on his gear and grabbed the ice axe, and soon he was on his way up the sheer mountain face. The progress was slow but sure. Just as he had thought, he *was* ready, and he climbed with skill and confidence.

About a third of the way up, a cloud descended, hovering just where Sam hung on the side of the mountain. Its thickness removed all visibility, lingering like a blanket, veiling the peak above and making it impossible to continue. Sam remained suspended in this spot for what seemed like an hour, but the cloud refused to lift.

As he assessed his options, his thoughts were interrupted by a shout. "Help! Please, someone help me!" a desperate female voice rose from the base of the glacier.

Sam shouted down, "I'm coming!" and he began making as rapid a descent as he could. Despite the already cold conditions, a glimpse from below sent an icy chill through his spine.

"Please come quickly!" the girl pleaded.

Sam dispensed with climbing the last fifteen feet, instead simply leaping down to the surface, where a lone journeyer stood with her back to the cliff while a ravenous wolf growled at her just a few feet away. The sound of Sam's fall momentarily scared off the wolf and he trotted away from them, still snarling.

"He's been stalking me," she said, "and I'm afraid he'll attack at any moment."

Sam looked over at the girl and gasped. It was Jill! But this was no time for introductions. Her life hung in the balance.

"Jill, can you climb?" Sam asked.

"I've never climbed on ice," she replied without taking her eyes off the menacing beast.

"I can teach you," he answered. Then, handing her one of his axes, he said, "You'll need this to protect yourself if he comes back. Wait here. I won't be long."

Keeping an eye out for the animal, he inched his way along the wall until he found the entrance to the small cave. He swiftly dove in and retrieved axes and crampons for Jill, and then emerged and returned to her side. He quickly instructed Jill to put on the spikes and verbally explained the technique. Just then, the wolf reappeared, prowling back and forth, emitting cruel-sounding noises and waiting for a moment of vulnerability. It looked gaunt and mean—and hungry!

Thrusting his axe out toward the beast, Sam said, "You'll have to go first while I try to keep this thing off of us. Once you're up a few feet, I'll follow you. I'll have to teach you as you climb. Do you think you can do it?"

"I think so. I'm a good climber, and a quick learner," she replied haltingly.

She turned to face the mountain, reaching up to insert one axe with her right arm and then pushing her right boot into the ice with as much force as possible. She repeated the procedure with her left arm and then pulled her left foot up. She was off the ground.

"Good," Sam encouraged her. "Keep going a little bit higher."

Meanwhile, the new developments seemed to anger the wolf. He roared louder, bared his teeth, and crept slightly closer.

"Hurry...if you can," Sam pleaded.

Jill was about eight feet up. Sam knew he had to make his own escape, so he let out a loud shout and thrust his axe close to the animal's face, and then he turned and quickly scrambled up to her side. The wolf seemed undeterred as it sized up the opportunity. Racing toward the cliff, it leaped high in the air, clamping its powerful teeth on Jill's right boot and digging its claws as best it could into the ice, but the traction was not enough. Jill's body jolted as one hundred pounds of weight thrashed angrily below her.

"Hold on!" Sam shouted, but she was slipping.

Her grip gave way, and she and the beast plummeted backward into the snow. The force of the fall separated them, and the big animal rolled backward, springing quickly to its feet and shaking violently as if slightly dazed. Jill was still on her back, but she could see the wolf as it measured the distance to its prey. It pounced toward Jill's exposed neck, hoping to make a quick kill with its powerful jaws. Reacting instinctively, Jill sat up and lifted her arms in front of her face, elbows bent and fists balled tightly.

Jill's movement had cut the measured distance by two feet, and her left elbow landed squarely on the wolf's nose. Jill once again fell on her back, but the blow to its nose momentarily slowed the attacking beast. Sam jumped from his perch, his heavy spiked boots scraping the animal's hind legs. It looked over at Sam, annoyed at the interruption, but turned quickly back to its original target. Sam somehow had the alertness to hang onto one of the axes. He rolled and jumped up just as the wolf leapt toward the still sprawled Jill. Sam had one chance and it was a risky one. He lifted the axe high over his head and swung it, aware of the danger of missing its mark and hitting Jill instead.

Swoosh. The axe dug deeply into the shoulder of the animal. It let out a screeching yelp, then slammed its jaws shut a mere fraction of an inch from Jill's neck. The wolf gave one last menacing look at Sam and Jill, and then, dragging the wounded appendage, shuffled off into the forest. Jill could no longer control her emotions, and she burst into tears. Sam did his best to console her, but he too was still trembling.

After a long time, they both stood up to dust themselves off. Jill looked at Sam and said, "Bio told me someone would be here waiting for me, to help me climb the glacier. Then I got here and there was no one. That wolf could have killed me. Where were you? Were you leaving without me?"

Sam's mind raced with a dawning awareness. He shouldn't have gone ahead. When Bio had said, "When I am ready for you, you will know," he had mistakenly assumed that Bio would come for him. Now he realized that this fellow journeyer was the signal. Bio had wanted him to wait, not because he

wasn't ready, but in order to help someone else—
someone who turned out to be Jill, the very person he
wanted to meet more than anyone else in the world.
His disobedience had almost cost her life!

Sam thought about making up a lie to cover his
wrongdoing, but he knew the best response was
to simply tell the truth. "I'm so sorry. Yes, I was
leaving. Bio had told me to wait, but I was too impatient. If I had known someone else was coming...I
hope you can believe me, but I truly didn't know.
I just assumed Bio didn't think I was ready for the
climb, and I knew that I was." He hung his head and
almost whispered, "I know it's a pretty lame excuse,
but it's the truth."

His honest response caught her by surprise. "I
appreciate your honesty. And, you *did* save my life,"
she said as she walked to his side and gave him a
warm embrace.

Sam was still a bit embarrassed, and all he could
say was, "I'm so sorry, Jill. I'm just glad you're OK."

She looked up at him curiously, "If Bio didn't
tell you anyone was coming, how do you know my
name?"

"Jill, I've wanted to meet you for so long." He
replied. "I'm Sam, and I saw you in the flat land. Do
you remember me?"

She looked intently at his face, and said, "I've
tried to block out every memory of that place, but
yes, I do think I remember seeing you once or twice."
Then shuddering, she added, "I'm so glad to be away
from there."

Sam nodded his head in agreement. He helped her take off her backpack, and then they moved inside the small cave where Sam made a campfire. While they rested and warmed themselves, they talked about their experiences in the flat land. Jill told Sam how she had never wanted to go there, but reluctantly had agreed to accompany one of her friends. Once they arrived, the friend, Julie, had immersed herself in the nightly rituals, leaving Jill alone. She only stayed in the flat land about two weeks, she told him, never really befriending anyone and never losing her dream of coming to the steep land.

"I can't explain it, Sam, but I just sensed there was a path to the sea. It took me several days to find it, but I never doubted there would be a way out," she said.

Sam told Jill all about Geo and the fight on the beach, and how Mr. Spencer had come with the boat to rescue him. He wanted to tell her much more about the first time he had seen her at the dock and that he was immediately attracted to her, and about all the times he had walked around looking for her, but he was too embarrassed. And he certainly didn't mention anything at all about Gina!

That afternoon, he took her to the smaller mountain and carefully repeated the training that Bio had given him. They practiced together the necessary techniques to conquer the icy climb that waited. He realized now that all the extra time he had spent in training allowed him to expertly teach his unexpected pupil.

As they made their ascent, he skillfully coached Jill and gave her encouragement when it seemed too hard to continue. It became quite obvious from her courage and demeanor that she had also spent time with Bio. She never complained, despite the level of difficulty. They finally made it to the top of the icy face and onto another plateau.

Bio was there, waiting for them, once again cooking fish over an inviting campfire. He greeted them with a loving embrace. Jill excitedly told Bio all about the wolf and how Sam had saved her, but Sam did not relish the tale. They ate dinner amid the picturesque setting, the sun quickly melting into the mountain.

Afterwards, Jill fell sound asleep, weary from the exhausting climb. Sam and Bio sat in silence for a moment, when Bio finally spoke, "Sam, I'm disappointed in you. I asked you to wait."

"I'm sorry, I just..." Sam fought for words.

"Sam," Bio smiled forgivingly, "The journey is not yours alone. You must journey individually *and* in community. I desire for many to come and meet me on this mountain, and I have chosen you to be a guide to lead others here. Your disobedience caused Jill unnecessary hardship—and almost her life."

Sam responded, "I don't really have any excuses for my actions. I'm genuinely sorry. I guess I thought I needed to be doing something. I felt like I was no longer making progress on the journey."

"I measure things differently than you," Bio intoned. "Progress isn't achieved by proving your own ability, but by doing my will." He added a few sticks to the bright orange coals and blew gently until a flame sparked upward. Then he looked up and smiled, "Sam, Sam, when will you learn that you have nothing to prove? My acceptance is unconditional, which is a good thing since you could never earn it. No one has to earn my love. I give it freely. You just need to receive me."

"But don't you care if I get stuck in the same place...not moving forward and climbing higher?" Sam asked.

"Sometimes progress means waiting on me, and doing what some would call nothing. There will be times when I am silent, but even during these days you must be vigilant, never ceasing to prepare for my call. Often, the small things I ask you to do are moments of preparation for receiving a task of great importance. Wait, listen and be ready."

In that instant of gentle reprimand, Sam felt love as he had never known it. He fought back tears. Bio still loved him, despite his failures. How could he not in return love this man who had saved him from the raging river, had walked with him and taught him so much on the journey, and now had asked him to be a guide for others? Sam felt so undeserving of this task, but Bio's sparkling, intense eyes told him otherwise.

Finally, after a few moments of silence, Bio added, "Oh, and Sam, I wanted you to wait partly because I thought you might enjoy meeting Jill." His smile broadened as he turned into his sleeping bag for the night.

Sam lay awake a long time thinking about another incredible day in the steep land. Despite his failure, he sensed the stain of disobedience and unworthiness being washed away by the powerful wave of forgiveness. The next day he rose to the pleasant aroma of strong coffee brewing over a fire, the perfect antidote to a chilly mountain morning. He felt free, as if some hidden shackles had been removed, and even his eyes felt clearer, or maybe it was just an illusion since the first thing he saw was Jill. Her beauty held its own even in the impressive majesty of the steep land, and he was impressed, too, by her strength and the courage she had shown during the previous day's ordeal. He only hoped that he would have a chance to make a better impression.

Chapter 11

The Rescue Mission

This was getting embarrassing. Too many times when Jill had glanced over at Sam, he tried to quickly avert his stare, but he just couldn't keep his eyes off of her, and surely she had noticed. And now she was smiling with the kind of expression that said she knew he was looking at her. Sam was generally shy around girls, but something about Jill made him even more so than usual. He had no clue how she saw him. Did she view him as just a friend, or could their relationship bloom into something more? He wondered if she even thought about him.

Slowly, Sam began to feel more at ease around her. They had many opportunities to talk and share stories of their childhoods, but they rarely mentioned the flat land. Perhaps they were still slightly uncomfortable discussing it with Bio so close by.

Later, they were joined by other climbers. Sam was disappointed at first, because it took away some of the one-on-one opportunities with Jill. But true to his word, Bio began training Sam to be a guide, several times leaving the group to his charge. Sam found his greatest joy was to lead and instruct others, and sometimes he would ask Jill to help him in this new role.

Bio often said to Sam, "If you want to lead you must be a servant. Watch me, and pattern yourself after what I do."

What Sam observed was a combination of strength and humility. Bio would usually start the day at the front of the pack, pointing out the way and recommending certain routes that would avoid the danger spots, but soon he would filter back, checking in with each climber as he walked alongside them for a stretch of the trail. Many times he ended the day at the back, where he kept a close eye on everyone and thus was able to aid any stragglers and provide encouragement and instruction.

Occasionally, Sam actually saw Bio carrying someone's load so that they could march forward without the bone crushing weight of their backpack. Sam marveled at Bio's strength, as he bore not only his own pack but also the weight of others' burdens. When the day's journey was ended, Bio usually allowed the weary travelers to sit while he made a campfire and cooked a meal. He continuously stressed the importance of proper nourishment and rest.

One time, however, Bio delayed his normal routine of preparation at the end of a long day. Instead, he simply sat by the fire, engaging in conversation with Jill. Several of the other girls decided to prepare the meal, and they began busily gathering firewood and cooking utensils, being pretty obvious about what they were doing, and making lots of noise to try to attract Jill's attention. Unsuccessful, one of them abruptly called out to Bio, and he rose to go speak to her. "Bio, would you please ask Jill to get up and help us?" she pleaded.

Sam couldn't hear the rest of the conversation, but the girl gestured broadly toward the other girls, and then glanced disdainfully at Jill. Bio patiently smiled as he allowed her to finish. Then Sam saw him place a hand on her shoulder and talk to her a moment before returning to resume his conversation with Jill. Clearly, Bio had told her that Jill was doing fine just where she was. Sam wanted to join them, too, but the intent look on Jill's face made him realize that whatever they were talking about was too important for him to interrupt.

Sam took it all in, and he tried his best to emulate what he had seen. He tried to exhibit the humble leadership style that Bio had demonstrated. He was quick to help, offering patient guidance to the less experienced travelers. Sam especially enjoyed walking alongside Jill, and the sound of her voice and the radiance of her face and eyes seemed to cheer him and give him added strength.

One day, though, Sam could tell that she was deeply troubled about something. "What's wrong, Jill?" he asked.

"I was just thinking about my cousin. He came here even before I did, but I found him in a meadow far below, too afraid to continue." Jill paused, and looked up hopefully at Sam, "His name is Kale. Do you know him by any chance?"

Sam looked at Jill incredulously. "Kale! Yes, I know Kale and I saw him there, too. He's your cousin?"

"Yes," she responded, choking back tears. "I wish we could convince him to join us. I want him to meet Bio and experience what I've felt and seen here on this mountain."

Sam paused momentarily, and then haltingly offered, "I'll go with you if you want to try."

She looked at Sam appreciatively, "You will?"

"Yes, in fact, I think I should. Bio said he wanted me to learn to become a guide to lead others. Maybe this is my duty, or calling, or whatever." Sam wasn't being falsely modest, but he was simply unaccustomed to thinking of himself as someone who Bio might use to accomplish his purposes.

Later, they spoke to Bio, and he seemed genuinely pleased at their desire to go help Kale. He called it a "rescue mission," and he blessed them as he sent them on their way. Leaving the group, the two of them began the long descent back down toward the meadow.

Sam enjoyed the chance to spend time with Jill. Now that Bio wasn't around, he brought up something that he had been reluctant to approach her about. "Jill, did you know much about me in the flat land?" he asked.

She laughed. "I was afraid of you at first. Everyone knew who you were and that you were

Geo's best friend and right hand man." Sam winced, but she continued, "But when I saw you one day on the street, I sensed that you weren't a bad person. I could just tell."

Sam was glad to hear that last part. He hesitantly offered, "I saw you, when you first came, and sometimes I looked for you."

"Really? I assumed hardly anyone even knew I was there. Why were you looking for me?" Jill asked innocently.

He wanted to tell her the truth…that he had been smitten by her beauty. His heart pounded and he hoped she couldn't see the veins bulging in his neck. He opened his mouth to tell her, but instead the following words came out, "Uh, I guess I heard that you wanted to come here to the steep land." Then he quickly continued, "I wonder how you were able to leave the flat land so easily when I had to literally fight my way out of there, and someone even had to come rescue me?"

Jill nodded her head and said, "Actually, I talked to Bio about that. He said that the longer someone stays there, the harder it is to leave. I was only there a couple of weeks, and never really bought into it."

Sam felt almost ashamed, but he admitted, "I was there a long time—too long. I never really felt right there, but it was easy to get caught up in it, and Geo seemed to make me a special target."

Jill replied, "Well, don't start thinking that I'm perfect or anything like that. I still feel badly that I left Julie behind. And I'm not a very patient person. I'm afraid I said some things that really hurt Kale."

She started to sob, and Sam waited until she could continue. "I'm so sorry for how I treated him when he refused to join me. I'm probably the reason he's still down there."

Sam gently touched her shoulder. "Hey, it's OK. You'll have another chance when we see him, and besides, you can't blame yourself for Julie's or Kale's decisions." Sam was secretly glad to see this side of Jill because he had, in fact, begun to think so highly of her that he could hardly conceive of her ever doing anything wrong. Maybe if she wasn't perfect she could overlook some of his failures.

Finally, they arrived at the plateau by the steep cliff. The banquet table stood empty, but on the far end Sam noticed rope and spikes. "Look," he said, "we can use these to repel down." With the aid of these unexpected resources, they soon emerged into the meadow, where they were greeted by the lonely sight of Kale standing next to the tiny hut that was now his home.

Jill ran to him and gave him a huge hug, saying, "Kale, I'm so glad to see you again."

Kale grinned broadly and held her tight. "Good to see you, cuz." Then looking at Sam, he added, "You two know each other?"

"Hey, Kale," Sam said and gave him a quick guy-hug. "Yes, we met not too long ago, just a little higher up from here."

"So what brings you back down?" Kale asked warily.

"We came to visit you," Jill replied. "And I needed to say I'm sorry for some of the things I said to you the last time I was here."

"That's OK," Kale shrugged. "I'm really glad you came. Sometimes it gets a little lonely."

They talked for a while as Kale prepared a place for his two unexpected visitors. Then he built a fire and cooked a simple meal of trout and wild potatoes. After dinner, he reached into his hut and pulled out a small, weathered guitar. "Would you guys like to hear a song I've been working on?"

"Sure," said both Sam and Jill.

It took Kale a few minutes to tune the strings, and then he shyly said, "This is a song I've been writing. It's not finished yet, but..." and his voice trailed off.

"Go ahead, Kale," Jill encouraged him. "You've always been gifted musically. I wish my side of the family had your gift."

Kale laughed, "Well, you haven't heard the song yet."

He cleared his throat and began to strum, singing softly:

> Praise the Maker of the mountains
> Dweller of the high places
> Draw me to your home
> I will follow when you call me
> Dwelling in the high places
> Bring me to your throne

Kale stopped, without looking at either Sam or Jill, and said, "It's not much, and I'm not finished yet, but I think it has potential."

Sam spoke first, "That's awesome, Kale."

Jill remained quiet, and then her eyes met Kale's. "I really like it, Kale. But one thing sort of puzzles me."

"What do you mean?" Kale asked.

"You're singing about following to the higher places, but you're living down here in the meadow."

"Well, yeah, I know," Kale began, "but I've heard about the mountains. Besides, it's just a song."

"Yes, Kale," Jill said, "but wouldn't you like to sing about something that you've really experienced?"

"Of course," Kale replied.

"Then let us help you climb, and let us take you to meet Bio. Do you know who he is?"

"Yes," Kale said. "I know all about Bio."

Jill responded gently and compassionately, "But you don't know him personally. Your music is beautiful and I think he would want you to know him so that you can write from your heart, not just from your head."

"Maybe so, but I told you before that I'm not climbing higher."

"Your song says, 'I will follow him,'" Jill reminded.

"It's just a song, OK?" Kale bristled. "If you came all the way down here just to try to make me go back with you, you wasted your time."

Sam motioned for Jill to back off, and then he said, "Hey, hey, you two. Settle down. Let's not

worry about that right now. Kale, I know one thing—
Jill really does love you. And when she mentioned
she was coming here, I volunteered to come with her
because I care about you, too. Thanks for sharing the
song, and now let's just enjoy some time together."
Then, looking at Jill, he continued, "No agendas and
no expectations. OK?"

Later, Sam pulled Jill aside as Kale was tending
the fire, and he told her, "Jill, we can't blow in here
and speak a few magic words and expect Kale to
come with us. We have to be willing to listen and be
his friend, even if he never leaves this meadow. Kale
is who he is, not who you want him to be. Sure, we
can hope to see him move beyond what he is today,
but we can't demand it. Can you put your expectations aside and simply spend time with your cousin?
Can you do that?"

"I don't know. It's hard for me, Sam. I'm the kind
of person who wants to see results," she sighed, "…
but I'll try."

So they spent the next couple of days catching
up and sharing stories. Sam finally got to go with
Kale to the fishing spot nearby, and they enjoyed a
pleasant day in the warm sun, even catching a few
trout. While they never directly brought up the topic
of Kale returning with them, he seemed very interested in their tales of adventure in the high places.
They told him about Bio, with Sam sharing the story
of falling into the raging river and Bio rescuing him
at the last moment, and Jill adding her tales about
the mountain of mirrors, the ravenous wolf, and her
frequent campfire chats with Bio.

One evening as they sat around the fire, Sam glanced at Jill and said, "I guess we need to start back up the mountain." Then looking over at Kale, he added, "Kale, it's been so good to spend time with you. You have a nice place here, and maybe we'll be back sometime to see you again."

Kale looked slightly surprised. "You're not going to try to convince me to go with you?"

Sam chuckled, "I'd love to do that, but that's entirely your decision." With full sincerity, Sam continued, "Of the three of us, at least you're the one who made the right choice that first day by coming here instead of going to the flat land. You're definitely better off here than if you'd gone there."

Kale sat silently for a moment, his defenses slowly crumbling away. Unexpectedly, he said, "I think I'd like to join you guys on the mountain."

"Really?" Jill replied hopefully.

Kale smiled at her and said, "Lots of people have come past me on their way up, and I always sensed their disapproval. This is the first time anyone has simply spent time with me without telling me I'm a failure for not climbing the mountain." Looking over at Sam, Kale added, "Thanks, friend."

* * * * *

Geo peered into the meadow, disgusted at what he had just heard. Nevertheless, a sly smile swept across his face, and he began to laugh. Who did this pesky trio think they were? When he thought about the surprise that awaited them, he reared back his head and howled his delight toward the distant moon.

The precious steep land! Ha! Geo salivated at the thought of disrupting the lives of even the ones who had come here. Obviously, he preferred to steer them into the flat land, but what good had the steep land done for Kale? Or for the Talkers or the Posers? Tomorrow he would once again make his presence known.

* * * * *

They made their plans, and the next morning they gathered up their gear and started up the trail. Jill couldn't contain her enthusiasm. "Kale," she said, "today you're going to see the *real* journey!"

At that very moment, something unexpected occurred. About fifty feet from the cliff, Kale suddenly stopped. Jill and Sam continued for a few paces, then turned and motioned for Kale to catch up.

"I can't" he said.

"Sure, you can," Jill answered. "We'll help you, Kale."

"No, really," Kale said with a quizzical look on his face. "I literally can't move forward."

Sam walked over to Kale. Grabbing his shoulders, he tugged, but he couldn't budge Kale. It was as if he had reached the end of an invisible leash.

It soon became apparent that some unseen tether was attached to Kale's brain. They could grab him by the legs and pull them forward, but his head would not budge past a certain point.

Finally, Sam said, "I think I know what's happening, Kale. Your fear of failure has created some sort of bondage that ties you to this place."

"I think—no, I *know* you're right, Sam," Kale admitted. "I've lived in fear for so long. I've tried to deny it and even cover it up, but it's true. I really want to leave the meadow and reach the high places, but...I don't know. Maybe my fear won't let me go."

Jill shook her head and asked, "What do we do now?"

Kale could only mutter, "I'm not sure."

They returned to the meadow, and sat silent for a long time, discouraged and rapidly losing hope. Kale wasn't in terrible shape, but many of his muscles, especially the ones he would need for the climb, had slackened due to the minimal effort required by the uneventful days he had spent here. Sam recognized it eventually, and his face brightened as he said, "I think I know the answer! You need to gain strength to overcome your fear," he said.

"Yeah, maybe that's it," Kale said. "I know I've been able to take life pretty easy since I've been here."

Sam and Jill began coaching Kale and encouraging him. For the next several days, they pressed him to push harder. He did stretching and limbering exercises daily, and strength conditioning every other day. Sam drew upon some of his martial arts training techniques, with Jill adding her knowledge of body control and dance to create a well-rounded regimen. The results were remarkable and clearly visible.

They excitedly set out for the cliff once again, approaching the pivotal moment apprehensively. Kale tried to step beyond the rope's previous length, but it didn't work. The invisible leash held tight at the same spot fifty feet from the cliff.

They returned dejectedly to the meadow. That night as they were sitting near the fire, Jill thought back to when she first met Bio on the mountain of mirrors, and she remembered that she too had been unaware of the nature of her need until he revealed it to her. The recollection gave her a thought. "I was just thinking," she began, "that maybe we've been trying to find a physical solution when what we need is not physical, but mental...or even spiritual."

Her words sparked something in Sam. Bio had said he would be a guide, and he was totally focused on the physical aspects of that mission. Maybe Jill was right and perhaps being a guide required more than just physical skills. Kale's condition was as much spiritual and mental as it was physical. "You're right, Jill," he began. "We've been so focused on developing Kale's strength. Our efforts have not been a waste of time, but now we need to focus on the spiritual. Kale, what you need is faith."

Sam and Jill began to share their faith with Kale. They spoke of the reality of the path and the journey. They spoke of meeting Bio and learning to trust him. Kale believed them and as his faith began to grow, he no longer accepted the meadow as his final destination, but believed that he was being called to a higher place. So they set out on the trail again, and this time

Kale made it past the previous boundary, but once again snapped to a stop only a few paces beyond.

Back to the drawing board. As they brainstormed around the campfire that evening, Sam said, "OK. Faith got us further down the path, so can we agree we're thinking in the right direction?"

"Sure," said Kale.

"But what's left besides faith?" Jill wondered out loud.

"Well, maybe stronger faith?" Kale offered.

"You either believe or you don't," Jill mused, "and, Kale, after the last few days, I really think you believe. Don't you?"

"Definitely!" Kale replied.

"I think I've got it!" Sam said enthusiastically. "We need to add hope. It's one thing to believe something is true in general, but you also have to be convinced that it's true *for you*. Hope can propel you past the temporary setbacks. When you hope for something and become certain of its eventual reality, you'll begin to act as if it's already happened."

So they began to offer Kale glimpses of what the mountain above was like. They described the spectacular vistas and the bounty of the banquet table on the plateau. Kale's heart beat faster in his chest as he visualized the splendor that awaited him, and hope grew inside his heart.

The next day, they broke camp to again approach the cliff. Treading carefully, they made it past the prior boundary. This time it appeared that he would break free, but about ten paces further than the previous day's stopping point, he slowed as each additional step required more force. It was as if the leash had limbered and was now an elastic band, but it finally tightened just a few feet from the cliff wall. Kale and Jill seemed distraught, but Sam authoritatively said, "Good! We're making real progress, Kale. Don't give up."

"OK, I guess," Kale said. "But what else can we do?"

Sam replied, "We're getting so close, but there must be one more missing ingredient. Does anyone know what it is?"

Kale shook his head, but Jill thought for a moment, and then said, "Love! We need all three — faith, hope and love."

Kale looked up with a question mark on his face. "Love? How can that help me?" he asked.

Sam replied, "She's right, Kale. I think your willingness to leave, and the progress you've made, shows you've already developed faith and hope. The missing ingredient is love. Love can carry you further than anything else. It brought Bio from his rightful place with his father to this mountain to meet with anyone who dares to come to him. Kale, Bio loves you, and he waits to meet you. Love is the element that can break down all barriers."

They returned to the camp and began to pour out love into Kale's heart. Jill's presence proved vital. She confessed to Kale that she had been conditional in her love. She reminded him of the times growing up when they had been so competitive, and she understood how Kale must have felt that he had to perform well to earn her love. She sobbed genuine tears of repentance and looked at Kale and said, "Kale, I love you. I really do, and I don't want you to ever again have to try to earn it. I love you for who you are. I love you right here in this meadow, even if you never climb higher."

Kale burst into tears as he related how he had always felt he didn't deserve love unless he did something to prove he was worthy. Even on this journey, he felt ashamed of only reaching the lowly meadow, and he assumed that only if he climbed to the top would he truly be loved.

Sam added his story of how he had failed Bio and almost caused Jill's death by his disobedience at the glacier, yet Bio had expressed unconditional love not only by forgiving him, but also by commissioning him to be a guide to lead others to the high places. Kale absorbed it like a sponge. They sobbed and laughed and prayed together by the warmth of the fire.

The next morning, they set off toward the cliff, collectively holding their breath when they approached the previous stopping point, and then exhaling together as Kale glided past it, finally untethered from the meadow. When they reached the edge of the steep ascent, Sam volunteered to climb up and secure the rope, but Kale insisted on going first. With surprising skill and ease, he led the way up.

* * * * *

Geo fought back the urge to let out an angry and anguished cry. He could not believe what he was observing. These three weaklings had managed to defeat him. Faith. Hope. *Love*. More words he would have to add to his banished list. Why did Bio love such frail and fickle creatures? He would never understand that.

He mulled the consequences of what had just transpired. While he did not relish admitting it, he knew that his attacks on Sam, Jill and Kale would now fall to a lower dimension. Their eternal destiny was sealed, and even he, the great Geo, could not snatch that away from them. Nonetheless, he could continue to confront them, no longer on the eternal plane, but on the temporal. He could make their lives as miserable and insignificant as possible. Bio may have won this last battle, but Geo remained the master at robbing and stealing one's joy, at destroying one's effectiveness.

Love. What a contemptuous word! Then a thought came to him, and he formed a sly grin. "Sam and Jill seem to be developing an attraction for each other," he thought. "Let's see if I can use that against them." He began devising a new plan. "I'm the great Geo," he announced to the empty meadow, "and I never give up."

* * * * *

The three young victors climbed the stone steps, where the banquet table was once again luxuriously decorated and provisioned. They feasted together and gave thanks for the power of faith, hope...and especially love. After a while, Bio came and personally greeted Kale with a warm and compassionate embrace. "Welcome, my son," he told him, and the two of them left together to celebrate and to climb.

"Are you disappointed in me for staying so long in the meadow?" Kale asked.

"Disappointed? No" Bio smiled. "I would never ask you to climb until you're ready. But it's not the mountain that holds you back."

"What do you mean?" Kale asked.

"When did you make your decision to begin the journey?" Bio asked.

"I've always known about the journey, from as far back as I can remember. I just assumed I was always a part of it."

"Kale, the journey is not a family tradition to be passed down. It's not a birthright. You must decide for yourself if you're willing to risk all for the journey."

Kale hung his head. "Obviously I'm not cut from the same cloth as my family. I feel like such a failure."

Bio replied firmly, but patiently, "Kale, this is not a test to be passed, even though it sometimes presents tests. It's a walk with a Person. I AM the journey; my Father presides over it, and my spirit gives witness to it. Will you follow me? Not your parents, not your grandparents, not your traditions, but me. Follow me."

Kale stood motionless for a moment, but then he lifted his head and peered into Bio's face. "Yes, I will. Even though I know I'll stumble, I will follow you. It's all I have left."

"Kale, this day you have truly embarked on the journey. You must never measure your walk against anyone else except me. Don't worry how high you go or how long it takes. Just walk where I lead you."

Chapter 12

The Valley of Echoes

Today would be the day. Sam could no longer stand it. He had to tell Jill how he felt about her, and he desperately wanted to know if the feelings were mutual. But every time he mustered the nerve, something happened; like yesterday when, just as he was about to speak, a noise from the bushes was followed by the emergence of the clan of Talkers, still making their way in a huge circle around the mountain. Jill was polite to them, but Sam simply stood off to one side, steaming that they had interrupted the perfect moment with their babblings and urgings to join them in the pursuit of enlightenment.

Sam was, of course, still physically engaged in the journey, but mentally everything revolved around Jill. His quest for the summit and his desire to dwell in Bio's presence were now pushed to a far corner of his mind.

The day began perfectly as he and Jill set out on the trail once again. Sam spotted the ideal setting just above, a beautiful ledge overlooking a lush valley where a stream played peek-a-boo behind a line of trees dancing in the wind. His heart raced with anticipation, and he began rehearsing the words he would say. Deep in thought, he let Jill take the lead as he imagined how she might respond. It was a risk, he knew, because he wasn't one hundred percent sure…but they had worked so well together and had become such good friends on the side trip to rescue Kale. Besides, she probably already suspected his feelings, and he needed to know if she felt the same way.

Jill was at the overlook now. "Wait a second, Jill, there's something I want to tell you," Sam said, sounding far more out of breath than the climb warranted.

But instead of waiting, she cried out, "Look, Sam! There are the others!" She bounded excitedly down the trail to re-join the group, and Sam could hardly contain his disappointment. Why hadn't he said something to her sooner? He was angry at himself, and he was angry at the other climbers. Halfway down, she stopped and quizzically asked, "What did you want to tell me, Sam?"

Sam rushed to catch up and seize this new chance. But just as he reached the ledge where she had stopped, she almost shouted, "Oh, my goodness. I think I see my father!"

* * * * *

Jill rushed down the hill and ran to embrace her beaming father.

"Daddy, you're here!" she exclaimed.

"Yes, Jill." He held up the leather bound book as if it were a great treasure, and added, "I couldn't stop reading."

"I want to read it too, then," Jill said.

"You definitely should," her father agreed.

"So, tell me everything!" Jill urged.

"OK. Let's see. I already told you that I had a sudden urge to read the book. At first, I tried to read it like a textbook. I wanted to chart things out and identify rules and formulas. But the more I read, it felt like a—this may sound unusual—a conversation."

"Really?" Jill responded.

"Yes, that's the only way I can describe it. I felt like I was having a conversation with the Author. And the words...have you ever heard the phrase: 'a picture paints a thousand words'?

"Sure, lots of times."

"Well, Jill, there's something different about this book. In this book, a word paints a thousand pictures. And when I finally came on the journey and met Bio face-to-face, I felt like I already knew him."

"I've met him, too, you know."

"Yes, he already told me. Jill, I'm so proud of you! And so is your mother."

They hugged again, and then Jill said, "What did she say?"

"I came with her full support, Jill. Well, she's not one hundred percent convinced yet, but she's very curious. She told me that since that day we talked about your journey, she's noticed a difference in me. Things are definitely changing in our family."

"So she stayed at home?" Jill asked.

"Actually, she has gone to visit your uncle Michael. It seems that they have lots to talk about," her father smiled.

"Have you seen Kale?"

"Yes, he and Bio rejoined our group yesterday. Kale told me how significant a role you've played in his life."

"Well, I'm part of the reason he stayed so long down in the meadow. I think my new friend, Sam, had the biggest impact on Kale." Jill replied.

"Ah, yes, Sam. I've heard a lot about him. Maybe you can introduce me," said Jill's dad.

"I will. I'm so happy you're here, dad," Jill smiled.

"Me, too. I guess it's never too late to begin the journey."

* * * * *

Sam struggled to rein in his conflicted thoughts. Of course, he was happy for Jill. How exciting it must be for her to reunite with her father and with her cousin while on the journey. Still, he regretted not telling her how he felt. And now the opportunity seemed to have slipped away since she spent almost all of her time talking to Kale and her father.

Jill, on the other hand, wondered what Sam had wanted to say. Actually, she suspected that she knew. "What's the deal with Sam?" Jill thought. "If he has feelings for me, why can't he just come out and say it?"

"Guys can be so...so ridiculous," she blurted out loud. She quickly looked around to make sure no one had heard her.

"OK," her thoughts continued, "I'll just have to hurry things along somehow." She decided that Sam needed a push, and maybe there was a way she could provide it.

* * * * *

There were other guys in the group, and they all seemed to take notice of Jill. After awhile, and without realizing it, Sam's old competitive instincts started to resurface. He began to compare himself with the others, especially one guy named Josh. In Sam's opinion, Josh paid entirely too much attention to Jill, as he always took the spot right next to her whenever they rested and right behind her whenever they climbed. To make matters worse, Jill seemed to enjoy Josh's company.

Sam couldn't stand watching her talking to another guy, so most days he moved past them and assumed the front position, occasionally looking back to check on her. He wondered if she noticed how skillfully and fearlessly he led, or if she even cared. More often than not, she wasn't looking, but was talking to Josh. That just made Sam push harder up the mountain, and Bio often called out for him to slow down.

Sam grew impatient with the others, especially anyone who lagged behind. When they expressed concern about a particularly difficult climb, or asked to rest for awhile before continuing, Sam flippantly pressed ahead, sometimes tempting danger. Since it was obvious he would not have the chance to talk to Jill privately, he instead set out to do everything he could to impress her.

One day, Sam held back, waiting to catch Bio's ear at the end of the long line of climbers. Jill was nearby, and Sam confidently spoke loudly enough for her to hear, "Thanks to you, Bio, I've become an expert climber. I'll never let you down."

Bio responded curiously, "Sam, do you seek to impress me?"

Sam, failing to understand the intent of the question, replied, "I'm just saying that I have mastered the skills you need of me."

"No, Sam. You're saying you've become better than others. Why do you insist on such comparisons? The attitude that will truly impress me is when you recognize the giftedness in others and find as much joy in their growth and success as in your own."

"But in order to lead others, I want to be the best," Sam countered defensively.

Bio's next sentence was a curious one. "Sam, you will soon travel through the valley of echoes."

Sam suppressed his curiosity and said nothing, thinking that compared to the heights he had already conquered, a valley wouldn't be very difficult.

The next day, Bio summoned Sam. "I'm leaving you in charge here, Sam, and I've asked Josh to help you. There are dangers ahead, so be careful to watch out for those who are still learning their way in this steep place."

"Of course," Sam brimmed with confidence, hiding his slight annoyance at the prospect of sharing leadership duties with Josh.

They continued up the mountain after Bio left. The first few days unfolded uneventfully as Sam brought up the rear, and Josh led at the front. Josh proved to be quite capable, which only served to further agitate Sam. So one day, Sam announced that he would lead and he asked Josh to bring up the rear. Jill marched along in the middle, and Sam was at least content that she was no longer chatting with his rival. Still, he wanted to do something spectacular to impress her.

Shortly after lunch, he spotted a cave entrance far above them. Sam loved caves, and they held a reputation for danger in the steep land. Maybe this would be his opportunity to do something daring and spectacular, so he ordered the others to take a short break, announcing his intentions to go exploring the dark cavern.

Jill seemed alarmed. "Sam, be careful," she said. "You're not going in there alone are you? Maybe Josh should go with you."

He looked back at her and laughed nonchalantly, "Don't worry about me. And I *definitely* don't need Josh's help." He scrambled quickly up the incline until he stood at the entrance. One glance instinctively told him that he shouldn't go in alone, but looking back toward Jill, he shouted down, "It looks good. I'll just be a couple of minutes."

The cave was divided into a maze of many chambers, some narrow and small, others room-sized caverns. After only a few steps in, the view was stunning. Stalactites reached down, icicle shaped rocks dangling from a high, dark ceiling. Milky colored drops of water formed on their pointed tips, dangling for many minutes before finally yielding to the inevitable pull of gravity. Their occasional drips broke the eerie silence.

As he wandered even further back, he could hear the faint sound of running water ahead, and his curiosity pulled him in its direction. The shouts of his concerned companions were soon beyond earshot. Yet he pressed on. The light from outside strained valiantly to reach the recesses of the cave, but the turns and corners eventually stopped its progress. Sam ventured until he found himself engulfed in utter blackness. He blinked, hoping that his eyes would adjust to the dark, but to no avail.

Turning to exit, Sam stumbled on the uneven surface, slamming his head against an unseen protrusion in the cave wall. He fell to the floor, unconscious for several seconds. Had he been able to think clearly, he would have stayed put, waiting for the others to eventually form a search team to rescue him. However, pride took charge of Sam's aching mind as he crawled along on his knees. Determined to rescue himself, he pushed deeper into the dark.

Suddenly, there was nothing beneath him. His body hurtled down a long, slippery shaft, and he braced for the bone crushing ending that he assumed awaited him in mere seconds. Surprisingly, it never came. Instead, he plunged into a deep pool of cold water, the force of his fall carrying him far below the black surface. Flailing wildly, he managed to reach air, still engulfed in thick darkness. It didn't take long for Sam to realize he was moving. He had fallen into an underground river! The speed of the river told him that he was proceeding not horizontally back into the mountain, but downward, carried lower and lower by the force of gravity. As he bobbed forward, the cave ceiling occasionally forced his head under the water. He would hold his breath longer than he thought possible before briefly emerging into a pocket of air.

This process repeated itself many times; too many to count, until Sam's body was finally deposited on a rocky ledge. Still shrouded in complete darkness, he carefully stood, raising his hands above him to ensure that he wouldn't strike his head on the unseen ceiling. The coldness of the water had served to restore his senses, and he desperately tried to formulate a plan. But nothing could alter the fact that he—the very one whom Bio had designated as a guide—was lost.

Moving along at a crawl pace, he used his hands to steer him along the wall of the cave. He felt several openings leading in different directions, but they all led to a solid wall. He remained still, tying to hear any sounds that might lead to safety, but he was met with absolute silence except for the sounds of the water.

He wanted to cry out for help, but something inside prevented him. Sam's pride had been painfully wounded but, unfortunately, not completely eliminated. He tried all the passages again, to no avail. He even tried climbing one wall completely in the dark, hoping he might reach other passageways higher up, but nothing materialized. He was desperate and tired as he crawled back to the ledge and lay down. There was no way to be sure how long he lay there since the total darkness afforded no means of measuring time. It could have been an hour or it could have been an entire day. He slept fitfully while hidden forces of evil and good waged battle on the torn terrain of his mind.

First, he dreamed that he had never left the flat land. He could see himself with Squinty Eyes and Geo, still living the effortless life of ease and comfort.

Then he dreamed that he was lost in the steep land, separated from his climbing companions, but still able to see them—one hundred of them gathered around a campfire, singing and laughing. Then in the dream, Bio suddenly rose from the middle of the group, peering toward the darkness. Then, obviously looking for something, Bio left the flock, now ninety-nine in number.

He finally awoke, opening his eyes, hoping beyond reason that somehow he would see light, but the thick blackness still greeted him. Lying on the ledge, he thought of simply plunging back into the underground river, but this time not coming up for air. The journey had merely teased him, leading him to this unexpected end. Just as he was about to throw himself back into the water, the last vestige of his pride surrendered. He wept uncontrollably and began to cry out desperately for Bio to rescue him once again.

* * * * *

Mr. Spencer woke up with a jerk and looked at the clock on the nightstand. It read 4:02 AM. Something pressed hard in his mind—Sam. He arose with a dawning awareness that Sam once again needed prayer. As he prayed, he shook his head and said, "No, Lord, please, not that place." Yet Mr. Spencer knew the stirring he felt was real, and he recognized the urgency.

Very soon, his reluctance gave way to resolve. He continued to pray fervently even as he prepared for the journey that awaited him. Looking down at the two eggs sizzling on the griddle, he reached for a few more slices of bacon. Where he was going, he would need the extra energy.

* * * * *

A rumble interrupted Sam's cries, shaking the ledge, a brief but definite quake. He held his breath, fearing another stronger tremor, but one never came. To his right, though, he heard the distinct sound of falling rocks, and a sliver of light snaked its way into the blackness. His heart pounded, sending a rush of adrenaline to his arms and legs, He scrambled toward the white beam and began removing the rocky debris the slide had created. Finally, he squeezed through a small opening, emerging from the cave and blinking rapidly to adjust his eyes to the sudden light. As he quickly took in his surroundings, he didn't know exactly where he was, but he had a pretty good idea. As Bio had predicted, he had arrived in the valley of echoes.

Sam's head throbbed, and the tiny droplets of blood oozing through multiple scrapes and bruises served as a vivid red reminder of his predicament. As he walked about in the valley and took in his surroundings, his heart sank. Just a short while ago he had been high up on the mountain, growing ever closer to the summit. How quickly things can change! Now he was alone in this valley, far away from the pinnacle. His energy was sapped, and he couldn't even tolerate the thought of climbing back again. In one act of stupidity and disobedience, Sam felt he had jeopardized everything.

The valley was narrow, more like a canyon than any other valley he had ever seen. It was neither pleasant nor picturesque, but rather foreboding. The sun hid behind the encasing walls for most of the day, creating an eerie light. Despite the lack of direct sun, it seemed that shadows lingered everywhere. A damp chill lurked about, the kind of chill that knifes through clothing into skin and bone. It was colder here than it had been inside the cave, and Sam began to shiver uncontrollably.

Why had he been so arrogant? He cried out, "I am such a fool," and it echoed back at him repeatedly, the sounds reverberating with a hissing fury. The words which had originated from his lips now rushed back into his ears, filtering through and flooding his mind with a dark depression. More words began to pour forth, for some strange reason no longer in the first person, but in the second. He yelled out, "You're not worthy," and "You will die in this valley," and the mountain walls eagerly shouted them back in reply.

For several days Sam wandered about yelling insults at himself which the valley of echoes dutifully repeated over and over again. His search for a path of escape had long ago given way to a state of resigned hopelessness. He was lost, and the bleakness of his situation seemed to validate the constant stream of words cascading down on him.

When the resounding sounds swelled to crescendo levels, Geo appeared. In the high altitude he had looked pale and uncomfortable, but here in the valley of echoes he exuded a far more imposing presence. He was clearly most at home in the lowlands and the shadows, but even here, he glanced about furtively, as if not fully at ease.

"Sam," Geo began, "why are you down here in this valley?"

Sam answered, "It was just an accident. I fell in a cave."

"Ha!" Geo laughed, "You fell? It was an accident? No, Sam," he continued, "You were never meant to come here. You're too weak for the steep places."

He stopped to allow the words to echo. Like plunging an enormous needle into an open wound, he then mercilessly administered a near-lethal dose of guilt and shame. He reminded Sam of every mistake he had made, both in the flat land and here in this place. The words sparked like firecrackers as they bounced back and forth off the canyon walls.

Geo added, "You don't belong here. You're not strong enough, and"—he paused, straining, but unable to say the Name, and then finally continuing—"your leader will never want you back. As for Jill, she could have loved you, Sam, but now she's finding comfort in Josh's arms, and she will never be yours." The mention of Jill name sent violent chills down Sam's spine.

Geo softened his tone. "Come with me, Sam, back to the flat land. In my land, I will make you a prince and I will be your champion. It's all you have left."

Sam knew the words were lies, but the more they echoed, the more difficult it became to deny them. Every negative thought became an arrow, careening back at him, a direct assault aimed at his faltering spirit. "You're too weak," the mountain sneered at him, over and over again. His mind finally succumbed to the weapon-words. Geo was right. He had been a fool to enter the cave, and now Bio would never want him back in the high places again, and he had lost Jill forever.

"Come back with me, Sam," Geo whispered, but even the whispers were magnified as they bounded back and forth between the narrow walls.

Chapter 13

Hope in the Valley

The act of surrender brought numbness, the total absence of sensory awareness that can easily be mistaken for comfort. Sam trudged alongside Geo, confused and disoriented in the company of his friend-foe. Geo did his best to console Sam, promising him a life of ease and a way to forget his pain when they returned to the flat land. That sounded faintly appealing to Sam, but in the next moment pangs of remorse stung his heart as he thought of the loss of the beauty he had found... in this place...in Jill...and especially in Bio.

A gloomy cloud settled over the valley, but Geo walked ever more briskly as the visibility lessened, seeming to prefer fogginess to clarity. He told Sam that they simply needed to traverse a dark pathway to a nearby beach, where a boat waited to ferry them back to his domain. A nervous grin smeared Geo's face, and he gripped Sam's arm tightly. "We need to hurry," he said intently.

Their shadows darted along in front of them, impossibly elongated caricatures that added a haunting aura to Sam's already depressed state of mind. His sullen thoughts recounted the highs and lows of the journey, and he wept silently at the stigma of failure that he knew would accompany him for the rest of his life. He had failed, and all he knew to do now was to return with Geo. As soon as he could, however, he vowed to extricate himself from that drab island and return home.

The thought of home added to Sam's depression. Maybe his parents and all the others had been right. Perhaps he would have been better off never embarking on the journey. The unfulfilled promises would linger as a bitter taste in his mouth forever. At best, he hoped to somehow create a facade to hide his disappointment. He would become like so many others in his town, never admitting any failure, but bragging and telling grand stories of adventure and success on the journey.

The further he walked with Geo, the more he began to rationalize his plight. Geo wasn't all bad. Despite his unpleasant traits, he had provided Sam some opportunities he wouldn't otherwise have had. Geo seemed to sense Sam's thoughts, and he said, "Sam, I know you've heard some awful things about me, and I'm sorry for the way I treated you at times, but I just wanted to spare you from the disappointment of this place. Trust me. It will be much better for you when we leave. You can rest again, and forget all the things that caused you to struggle."

"I just want to see Jill again," Sam muttered dejectedly.

"Sam, you need to let go of Jill. You can't have her. But I have someone else in mind for you."

"Don't bother," Sam protested. "You can't trick me twice with Gina."

Geo laughed. "Who said anything about Gina? I'm talking about someone else—one of the finest girls the flat land has to offer."

* * * * *

Squinty and High Heels rushed to the table where Julie was sitting, ignoring the young men on either side of her.

"Julie," High Heels gasped breathlessly. "Time to celebrate!" as she picked up a drink and held it high.

"What are we celebrating?" asked Julie.

Squinty gave his best "get lost" look at the two guys, who grudgingly stood and moved away.

"We have a guy we want you to meet. Well, actually, Geo has him and is bringing him back tonight," High Heels said.

"Bringing him back?" Julie asked.

"Yes. Geo went to the steep land and found Sam."

"Who's Sam?" Julie asked excitedly, although the name sounded vaguely familiar.

"Sam is Jill's boyfriend—or was. But now he's on his way back here, and Geo says you'd be perfect for him."

Julie's jaw dropped. What an opportunity! She would steal Jill's boyfriend, and it would be such sweet revenge. By now, the mere mention of Jill's name almost made her sick. And she had grown even sicker hearing about the pompous steep land. Yes, this news was indeed cause for celebration.

"What does he look like?" she asked, trying hard to conceal her tingling emotions.

"Oh, he's definitely good-looking. But you'll have your work cut out—he's still in love with Jill."

"Hmmm," Julie smiled, "we'll see about that."

* * * * *

Geo continue talking as he guided Sam along. "You'll feel better when we get away from this place. I told you long ago that the steep land isn't everything people try to make it out to be."

"I remember," Sam said, and then he added somewhat defiantly, "You said it might not even be real, but that was a lie."

Ignoring the insult, Geo replied, "What is reality, Sam? I tell you what it is. It's what you *have*, not what you *want*. Forget all your silly dreams. Forget Jill, and forget the steep land. You tried but failed— no harm in that. But now it's time to accept what *you* can achieve, Sam. Why keep thinking about things that only end up disappointing you?" Pausing for effect, he added, "And like I said, I have the perfect girl for you."

"What are you talking about, Geo?" Sam asked.

"Did you ever meet Julie?" Geo replied.

"Julie—Jill's friend?"

"Yes, and I believe you'll find she is far more attractive than Jill."

"I could never do that," Sam said. "Do you think I'm stupid?"

Geo tightened his grip around Sam's arm, closing so tightly that Sam cried out in pain. "Don't disrespect me, Sam!"

Sam crumpled to the ground, but quickly rose, still defiant. Geo said something else, but in his disoriented state Sam didn't really hear it. He turned to look at the source of the unintelligible words, and the gray eyes that reflected back caused him to shudder. He wondered if his own eyes now resembled those of most of the people in his hometown, saddened and wearied from a life of mediocrity and defeat. Sam tried to say something, but his words were slurred and syrupy. Geo walked just behind him, gripping one arm and holding him up, his facial expression growing ever more delighted as Sam's motor skills slowly deteriorated.

Geo suddenly stopped, and he grabbed Sam's other arm and wheeled him around so that the two of them were face-to-face. "Bow down!" he said sternly.

"What?" Sam stammered incredulously.

"Bow down, Sam. I want you to bow before me and swear allegiance," Geo commanded.

Sam felt himself going down, against his will, with Geo applying pressure now to his shoulders and shouting, "Bow down. Bow before me," as the canyon once again echoed the words. Sam's weakened defenses teetered on the verge of collapse, and his knees had slightly buckled when he saw smoke rising in the distance. Another campfire! He thrust his arms skyward, breaking Geo's grip on his shoulders, and he instinctively stumbled toward the fire, despite the loud objections of his adversary.

A lone figure hunched over the flame, warding off the chill. When he saw them, he rose quickly and rushed toward Geo, shouting, "Leave him alone, Geo." Sam already knew in his heart what his eyes now confirmed. It was Mr. Spencer!

Geo laughed loudly and held his ground. "Why are you here, Spencer? Don't you remember this valley and what it represents? You couldn't even save your own family. Are you going to save Sam now?"

Mr. Spencer grabbed his chest as if he had been struck by a forceful fist. He coughed, and his speech became slurred, much like Sam's. He stumbled backward, holding up a hand, and said, "Be gone, in the name of…," but his voice cracked, and gurgling sounds were all that emerged. Confusion and guilt swept through his mind. He looked around with vacant eyes, and he could no longer quite remember why he was here. Geo's taunts echoed back and forth, and Mr. Spencer shuddered as painful memories locked away deep in his brain made their way to the surface.

Geo laughed even harder, and rushed over to Sam, who had fallen to his knees, and hoisted him onto his back. Turning to a choking Mr. Spencer, Geo kicked him square in the back so that he fell face first onto the ground. For a moment, Geo pinned him there with his right foot pushing hard between his shoulder blades. Finally relenting, he disdainfully said, "Forget about him. He's nothing. Let's get out of this place."

* * * * *

Bio looked on approvingly from his hidden perch as Jill took charge. She gathered into a tight circle with her father and Kale and a few other close companions, and they began to pray fervently, crying out for Sam's safety. Her heart pounded intensely, and she hoped that Sam was all right since she couldn't help thinking that the current situation was partly her own fault. She had been intuitively aware of Sam's feelings toward her, but instead of talking to him directly, she had flirted with Josh. It had been done innocently, she had convinced herself, but she knew that it must have driven Sam crazy.

No time to regret the past, she thought. She remembered her conversation with Bio on the mountain of mirrors. Yes, maybe she had acted foolishly, and certainly Sam's pride had tripped him up, but no situation, no weakness was beyond the reach of grace.

She closed her eyes even more tightly and lifted her hands pleadingly, a tear streaming silently down her cheek.

* * * * *

Mr. Spencer sat upright and felt a sudden surge of prayer-fueled energy. Geo and Sam were still in sight. He struggled to his feet and sucked in all the air he could, and then shouted, "I was saying, Geo... BE GONE IN THE NAME OF BIO."

When that magnificent name emerged from his lips, it jetted silently through the forest and into the canyon. It crashed against the wall with ear-splitting thunder. The mountainside rumbled, and a large pane of rock literally shattered and disintegrated as the name above all other names echoed back across the landscape. Over and over again, nature repeated the sound...Bio...Bio...Bio. Every animal, every bird, and every creature stood still and silent. Though encased in shadows moments before, sunlight burst forth in the valley, and in an instant the gray skies became brilliantly clear as light searched every corner and every crevice.

Geo's arms fell harmlessly to his side, and Sam slid down his back like a kid on a playground. Geo retreated rapidly, appearing frail and frightened, like a dog with its tail tucked. When the echoes ceased, Geo was gone.

Mr. Spencer limped toward Sam, placing his arm around him and shepherding him back to the campsite, where they sat in silence for several minutes as Mr. Spencer added wood to the fire. Finally, and without looking up, he began speaking quietly. "I know this valley well, Sam. Something happened long ago..." he looked up at Sam momentarily, then returned his gaze toward the fire and continued. "It was a rainy night. I was working late at the office, so my wife and daughter went without me to a piano recital. I've often thought that if I had been there..." his voice trailed off and he remained in thought for a moment. He shook his head slightly, then continued, "As they were driving home, my wife lost control and went into a skid, crossing the median. There was a head on collision," another pause. "They both died instantly." He looked up. His eyes shimmered with the hint of tears, yet somehow retained their familiar sparkle.

"Sam," Mr. Spencer finally uttered, "Don't lose hope. We all make mistakes, and, yes, there are consequences, but there is also hope. After the accident, I spent many days here in this valley. I was lost, and I blamed myself, but mostly I blamed Bio. I'm ashamed to admit it, but I talked with Geo and seriously considered leaving with him for the false comfort of the flat land. Only grace saved me. Bio came here, to this very spot, and he showed me that there was still a purpose for my life. He told me that what appeared to be evil and terrible, he could make good. What seemed to be defeat, he could fashion into victory. Sam, he even gave me a task that day. He asked me to return home and be an encourager. He promised to replace my sorrow with his joy, and to use my story to help others. I've tried to do that as best as I can."

Sam fell to his knees and sobbed, his tears a watery mixture of release and gratitude. When he was finally able to speak, he said, "Mr. Spencer, you've rescued me twice from the grip of Geo. I'd say you've done exactly what Bio called you to do. How can I ever thank you enough?"

Mr. Spencer shook his head slowly and said, "I can't explain what's happened with me and you, Sam. I've never done anything like this before. Ever! I returned home after Bio came to me in this valley, but mostly I've been a behind-the-scenes person. I just pray for people, and often they never know it. I sometimes wonder if …" he paused again, but finally finished the sentence, "I wonder if my life has really mattered. That's why what I've done with you is so…so unexpected…and so rewarding."

"Your prayers have probably made the difference in many, many lives, Mr. Spencer," Sam replied.

"I hope so," the older man smiled. "When Bio told me my story could be used to help others, I guess I assumed it would be something big and dramatic. Yet I've never written a book, never been on television, never been famous, but I've tried to always honor him. I don't know…maybe I've helped a few people in some way."

The sound of soft footsteps pressing down on the twigs and leaves preceded another voice, "Eight thousand, three hundred and fifteen…" It was Bio.

Mr. Spencer looked up with both joy and puzzlement. "Bio! What…what do you mean?"

Bio knelt down and placed one hand on Mr. Spencer's shoulder. "Eight thousand, three hundred and fifteen. That's how many people your life has already impacted. And Sam here is one of them," Bio said.

"I—I don't understand," Mr. Spencer said, shaking his head in disbelief. The number seemed so incomprehensible Bio may as well have said one billion.

"There are many things you never see, John," Bio responded. (It was the first time Sam had ever known Mr. Spencer's first name). He continued, "I ask my servants to sow seeds, but it is I who make them grow. John, your prayers have sown many seeds that have multiplied beyond your awareness." He let that linger for several seconds, and then added, "There are other seeds you've sown as well. Do you remember the two young men from that impoverished nation who had enrolled in a college near your home...the ones who needed a place to stay until their dorm room became available?"

John answered, "Yes, but they only stayed with me for three weeks."

Bio smiled. "They learned more from you in those three weeks than they learned in an entire semester at the college. Now, one is a pastor in his country and the other has started a school to educate and train others for ministry. The simple seed that was sown by you has produced fruit one hundred fold, and that fruit has in turn produced other offspring. And there are more stories much like that one." Pausing again, he looked at Sam, then back at John, "I think your number may be increasing many times more."

John Spencer could no longer hold back the tears. Sam stood and walked around to John's other side, placing his arm around him, saying "Bio's right. I wouldn't have survived without your prayers...and your action."

Looking across John's hunched back, Sam made eye contact with Bio, but quickly looked away, saying, "I'm so sorry."

Bio quickly responded. "Sam, I love you," he said.

"How can you still love me?" Sam began, but Bio held up a hand with such authority that Sam stopped in mid sentence.

"Do you love me, Sam?" Bio asked.

"Yes, of course I love you," Sam replied.

"Then guide my flock," Bio said.

Chapter 14

The Summit

The fire burned all night, and the three men never slept, their conversation laced with joy and laughter that sometimes only a campfire can summon. When morning came, Bio stood and said to Sam, "Come, you've been here long enough."

"Is Mr. Spencer—I mean, is John coming with us?" Sam asked, hoping he would say yes.

Bio replied, "He is welcome, but he has already seen what I will now reveal to you."

John stood next to them and said, "I think I'll be going back now. I'm sure you two have much to discuss." He said goodbye, and then Sam was once again alone with Bio.

Like the day before, long shadows accompanied Sam and his companion, but this time they danced along with joy as he and Bio moved briskly back toward the mountain. Soon, the two men emerged from the misty valley and resumed their climb, traveling far faster than before. In what seemed like no time at all, they were back among the high places, the canyon of echoes far below them. They were quiet for a long while.

Sam broke the silence when he said, "I know I'm forgiven, but I feel so unworthy to be a guide."

Bio shook his head and smiled, "Your ability to guide will come from me, Sam, not from yourself. Did Geo tell you to accept and be content with what *you* can achieve?"

"Yes," Sam replied, not at all surprised that Bio knew.

"Sam, I still want you to lead others, and I'll give you the strength to do it if you'll let me. With my strength, my spirit within you, you can do far more than you ever believed to be possible."

Sam dropped to his knees with gratitude, looking up at Bio. He wanted to say, "Yes! Yes! I'll let you," but all he could do was nod his head vigorously, clutching the feet of the merciful, magnificent man who stood over him.

When he had regained his composure, Sam asked, "What happened to Geo back there? Where did he go?"

Bio smiled and said, "He has no authority over you. He will occasionally try to claim it, but be assured; he will never wrestle you from my hand."

"Yes, but why did he just vanish without another fight?" Sam wondered out loud.

"Prayer is a mighty weapon, Sam, and many prayers have been offered up for you." Then Bio added, "Sam, do you remember when you called out to me in the cave?"

"Yes," Sam replied.

"Your cries for help occurred at the very moment both Jill and Mr. Spencer were interceding for you. The combined strength of those pleas reached my ears and literally shook the mountain. Don't ever let anyone try to convince you that prayer is not a weapon of action."

Sam dreaded asking the question rising up in his heart, but an even greater need to know finally compelled him to speak. "Is Jill still here on the mountain?"

"Jill's journey has continued, Sam. First, find your joy in me."

Tears formed in Sam's eyes, and he simply nodded, unsure if his path and Jill's would ever cross again.

Bio and Sam continued their hike together until they came to a vast chasm which separated them from the summit above. They walked to the edge and peered across, and then down. Sam could see no bottom, just an empty space between them and their destination.

"What do you see, Sam?" Bio asked.

"I see a great gap." Then after thinking for a moment, Sam continued, "This is the place you told me about after I had met the Talkers, isn't it?" Bio nodded, and after another moment of reflection, Sam said, "I believe you brought me here to show me the way across."

"You're catching on, Sam," Bio smiled. Then he led him to a place where a lonely tree formed an arch over the chasm. It was solid brown, except for sprinklings of dark crimson. "I laid this bridge long ago, Sam, and anyone who trusts me may cross it. All who come to this summit must pass this way."

They crossed, and when he looked back, Sam noticed that the sun shone down in such a way that the tree-bridge formed the shadow of a cross.

* * * * *

3 days later…

Sam paused and allowed his lungs to draw deeply from the cool, pure mountain air. The summit stood less than a hundred yards away now, and the rugged approach gave way to a much smoother bald knob. He took in the eagle-wing views, giving thanks for the privilege of this journey.

He had come a long way, and experienced many struggles and even more victories. The summit at one time had represented the end destination, the goal of his journey, but he had long since come to understand that his apex had occurred much earlier, when he met a rescuer with radiant eyes at the end of a rope in a swirling stream.

He was climbing alone again, but with the sense that Bio's presence went with him. He looked forward to this day with its rare majesty. Bio had said that few took the journey, and fewer still relished this moment at the summit of the steep land. Yet Sam's journey would not end here. Bio told him that even though he would return many times to guide others on their journey, Sam's journey would also take him back home to be a beacon of hope. In the tradition of Mr. Spencer, he would be a seeker and supporter of others willing to risk the rarified mountain air rather than settling for the sameness and mediocrity most were too willing to accept in the low places.

Adjusting his gear one final time, Sam pressed up toward the top. About fifty yards ahead, he noticed a lonely tent securely fastened on a small ledge and flapping in the mountain wind. With the sound of his approaching footsteps, someone emerged. It was Jill!

She smiled broadly and exclaimed, "Sam, I was hoping it would be you," as she rushed toward him. They embraced, and she noted the quizzical look on Sam's face. Smiling, she said, "Bio told me to wait here. He said he wanted me to climb to the summit with someone who would be coming behind me." She paused, and then added, "I'm glad it was you."

"Me too," he stammered, and then wanted to kick himself for not coming up with something more profound than that.

"What happened to you, Sam?"

"I was stupid. I shouldn't have gone so far into the cave alone, but I wanted to impress you." He pulled off his backpack and asked, "Can we sit down for a minute?"

"Sure," she replied, and they sat near the door of the tent.

Sam continued, "I guess maybe the main thing I've learned on the journey is that my whole life has been spent trying to impress people. I felt like I didn't quite measure up, but my pride caused me to try harder and harder to be better than anyone else. Until I met Bio, I never realized I could be loved just for being who I am." He looked at Jill's eyes, briefly then lowered his head and continued. "Anyway, back to the cave…I ended up in a valley—a terrible place that reminded me of all the wrongs I've ever done. Then Geo came and—"

"Geo? He was here?" Jill asked.

"Yes. Not up here, but down in the valley. He convinced me to turn back to the flat land with him."

"You were going back there?" Jill gasped.

"I thought I had to. It felt like I deserved it after all the mistakes I've made. Geo convinced me that I wasn't cut out for the steep land."

"Oh, Sam, surely you knew Bio would forgive you."

"I know, but it's kind of hard to remember that when you're in the valley."

Jill nodded, and then Sam continued, "Geo said something else you'll want to know. He told me to forget about you, that I had lost you forever. He had another girl in mind for me—Julie."

"Julie? My Julie?"

"Yes."

Now it was Jill's turn to lower her head, "So, she's still there. I worry about her."

"It's OK to wonder how she's doing, but you can't blame yourself, Jill."

Jill looked up, "I know. I just…I just feel responsible. Why didn't I make her come with me?"

"Jill, do you really think she would have come here?" Sam asked gently.

"No, I suppose not," Jill sighed. "I guess all we can do is pray. I prayed for you…a lot"

Sam smiled, "I know. Bio told me. Thanks, and I really mean that because it saved my life." He paused. "Keep praying for Julie—it may save hers, too."

After a few moments, Jill stood and said, "I've waited here like Bio said, but now I'm ready to go to the top. Are you?"

"Definitely," Sam smiled.

They walked in silence after that. Then, a few minutes later, they reached the crest, where a simple, open structure occupied the center of the summit, a terrace with a roof supported by four stone columns. At one end, a fire pit provided a welcome glow. In the middle of the terrace was a table boasting a feast like no other, much more elaborate than the one they had enjoyed on the plateau far below. As they walked toward it, Jill squeezed Sam's hand. Looking around, she marveled, "Look how beautiful it is!"

Sam remained silent a brief moment, and Jill walked on ahead onto the terrace. An uncontrollably broad smile swept over his face as he replied, "Yes, it really is beautiful."

Epilogue

15 years later…

S arah eagerly awaited the next day's arrival. She had just turned twenty-one, and had decided to take the journey. Only one or two of the others in her town would be going. Most said that they didn't want to be bothered with something that was probably a myth anyway. But Sarah was different. To her, it felt as if something, or perhaps someone, was calling her.

It was slightly annoying to her that, on this final day before her journey began, she had to go to the funeral of Mr. John Spencer. Sarah's mother wanted to attend, but she couldn't drive due to a cast on her leg from a recent injury, so Sarah would need to take her. When they arrived, the church was already brimming to capacity. "This man must have impacted a lot of people," Sarah thought.

The ceremony was simple and sincere. Three men spoke—the pastor first, followed by a distinguished educator from a small, remote country. The pastor spoke of the kindness and influence of Mr. Spencer, and how he had demonstrated his faith through both words and actions. The other man told how John's wisdom and generosity had opened up doors for education and training of literally thousands of young men and women on his continent. No one in the town seemed to have known that he had served on the Board of Directors for the ministry and had even donated generously to keep it growing in the last few years.

Then Sam Whitten rose to speak. He carefully placed his notes on the podium and then looked up at the overflowing crowd. "John Spencer was in many ways an ordinary man," he began. "He was a businessman who worked faithfully, with excellence and integrity, for the same company for many years. Many of you in this room today worked alongside him and can attest to his enthusiasm as he demonstrated that he was serving a higher calling, not just a job."

"Others of you knew him in a different way. Yes, his life included great tragedy with the untimely loss of his wife and daughter in a terrible accident. Such events could easily have derailed a lesser man, but John Spencer showed us how to turn apparent defeat into victory. His heart, though broken, emerged stronger through that experience, and it began to beat for the needs of others. You've already heard one story of how he opened his home and unwittingly blessed a continent. You know that he was a great encourager, always quick to share praise or a word of loving concern."

"I personally knew him as a great prayer warrior. I experienced personally the power of his prayer, beginning with a time of desperate need during my journey fifteen years ago."

Sarah's ears perked up when he mentioned the journey. Sam continued, "John Spencer was older than I, but we became like brothers. He had a knack for praying for me at the moments of my greatest need, and several times he even put action to his prayers by coming to help me when I couldn't overcome on my own. Over these last fifteen years, I've watched John and have come to know him not only as a friend, but for what he truly was. Anyone who ever peered into his vibrant, sparkling eyes knows that he was by no means just an ordinary man. His faith and his faithfulness made him truly extraordinary."

Sam continued for a few more minutes, pausing several times to wipe his eyes with his handkerchief. When he sat down, there was complete silence, broken only by the muffled sounds of an entire congregation choking back tears of memory and appreciation for a great man.

After the service, Sarah left to get the car and bring it around to pick up her mother by the door. As she walked, she saw Mr. Whitten and his beautiful wife. She hesitated, but then approached them.

"Mr. Whitten," she began, "Hi. Do you remember me? I'm Sarah, and I just wanted you to know I appreciated your words today."

Sam turned and smiled. "Thank you, and of course, we remember you, Sarah. And I'm sure you remember my wife, Jill."

Jill added, "Hi, Sarah, how's your mother?"

They exchanged small talk for a brief few minutes, and then Jill asked, "Sarah, did I hear that you're going on the journey?"

"Yes! I'm so excited and I can't wait. In fact, I leave tomorrow." Sarah replied enthusiastically.

Sam and Jill responded with genuine interest, and asked some very intriguing and perceptive questions. Unbeknownst to Sarah, they had been observing her for some time, and had even anonymously given the financial support that allowed her to attend some of the church youth trips. As Sarah spoke to them, she thought, "There's something different about them." Searching their faces, she finally noticed what it was. Both Sam's and Jill's eyes sparkled with depth and emotion, and even adventure, that she rarely saw in others.

They talked another minute or so, with Sam and Jill both offering good wishes for the journey ahead. As she turned to leave, Sam called back after her, "Sarah." She turned, and he continued, "Sarah, I just want you to know... we'll be praying for you."

Acknowledgments

I wish to thank…

My wife, Bev. Thanks for being the perfect partner in every way, for your support and insight, and for being such a great intercessor. You're my best friend, and I've thoroughly enjoyed our journey together.

My son, Reese, for your valuable technical help with the fight sequences. Your black belt in tae kwon do definitely came in handy for my writing!

My son, Grant, for taking that great picture in Scotland that became the design for the cover of this book!

Melissa Carlsen for your skillful editing and helpful suggestions.

Leigh Hicks for editing and proofing work on the early drafts.

Musical artists whose songs spoke to me, with lyrics rich in imagery: Jill DeZwaan, for "Coming Home;" The Robbie Seay Band for "Shine Your Light;" and Jill Phillips for "Sacred." Those songs stirred my imagination, and such stirrings are the seed of inspiration.

Also by Rick Brown

Out of the Forest:
Re-Engaging in God's Call to Purpose

Does your life exhibit the abundance and adventure Jesus described, or are you trapped in a safe, untested and monotonous existence? In his award-winning book, *Out of the Forest: Re-Engaging in God's Call to Purpose*, author Rick Brown explores an obscure but profound passage found in 2 Samuel 18:8. Describing a battle during Absalom's rebellion, the Scripture says: "The battle spread ... and the forest claimed more lives that day than the sword." With wit and encouragement, Brown discusses some of the reasons people are still running to their own forests, and provides hope for re-emerging into a life of purpose.

"Rick has fired a literary flare in the air, announcing a way out of spiritual mediocrity for all those who have somehow lost their way. Practical, insightful and grounded in a consistent life, Out of the Forest is a clarion call to reconnect, renew and realize."

Neil McClendon, Lead Pastor, Grand Parkway Baptist Church, Sugar Land, Texas

"Rick's book will challenge and encourage you. I especially love the Chapter on finding beauty...that's so important for the church. And I laughed out loud at the story of 'the nod.' This is good stuff!"

Robbie Seay, Worship Leader and Recording Artist

"I have witnessed directly Rick's commitment to front-line action and the depth of his spiritual character. Who better then to pen this stirring call to arms? I recommend it to you—into your corners and come out fighting!"

Jon Burns, Pastor in England and National UK Director for More Than Gold, London 2012 Olympics, England

Contact Rick Brown at rlbrown1234@gmail.com